ESSENTIAL

CAPOEIRA

THE GUIDE TO MASTERING THE ART

ESSENTIAL

CAPOEIRA

THE GUIDE TO MASTERING THE ART

Mestre Poncianinho
with Michelle Porter

BLUE SNAKE BOOKS
BERKELEY, CALIFORNIA

Published by New Holland Publishers (UK) Ltd and
Blue Snake Books/Frog, Ltd

New Holland Publishers Ltd
London • Cape Town • Sydney • Auckland
www.newhollandpublishers.com

Blue Snake Books/Frog, Ltd. books are distributed by
North Atlantic Books
P.O. Box 12327
Berkeley, California 94712

Reproduction by Pica Digital Pte Ltd, Singapore
Printed and bound in Malaysia by Times Offset (M) Sdn Bhd

Essential Capoeira: The Guide to Mastering the Art is sponsored by the
Society for the Study of Native Arts and Sciences, a nonprofit
educational corporation whose goals are to develop an educational and
crosscultural perspective linking various scientific, social, and artistic
fields; to nurture a holistic view of arts, sciences, humanities, and
healing; and to publish and distribute literature on the relationship of
mind, body, and nature.

1 2 3 4 5 6 7 8 9 — 13 12 11 10 09 08 07

Library of Congress Cataloging-in-Publication Data

Ponchianinho, Mestre.
    [Capoeira]
    Essential capoeira : the guide to mastering the art / by Mestre
Ponchianinho.
       p. cm.
    Originally published: Capoeira. London : New Holland Publishers, 2007.
    Summary: "An explanation of the aims, benefits, history, and origins
of Capoeira, Essential Capoeira introduces Capoeira Regional and
Capoeira Angola techniques and gives an introductory explanation of
the Game, the hierarchy within capoeira, the mestres, and the grading
system"--Provided by publisher.
    Includes index.
    ISBN-13: 978-1-58394-196-6 (trade paper)
    ISBN-10: 1-58394-196-7 (trade paper)
 1. Capoeira (Dance) 2. Capoeira (Dance)--History. I. Title.
    GV1796.C145P66 2008
    793.3'1981--dc22
                              2007021515

DISCLAIMER

AUTHOR'S ACKNOWLEDGMENTS

This book would not have been possible without the help of some special people. To my students Baris Yazar, Morris Reyes, Molinha, Katie Ellwood, Isabelle Schoenholzer, and Cientista—thank you for all the effort you put into your training, for the different ways you helped make this book what it is, for always being dedicated, and for being my friends. Also to my best friend, Contra-Mestre Casquinha, for helping me with this book and contributing some great pictures. Thanks to my dear wife Louise Almeida, who has supported and helped me in everything I do. Thanks also to Michelle Porter for her research and great writing. A big thanks to Cordão de Ouro, London, for always being with me, and always supporting this beautiful and precious art of Capoeira. And the most special thanks of all to my Mestre, for teaching me the wonderful, the ever-mystifying, and always revelatory art of Capoeira.

CONTENTS

1 Introduction 8

What is Capoeira? An explanation of the aims and benefits of the sport, along with its history and origins.

2 Development 14

Introducing the two main styles of Capoeira (Capoeira Regional and Capoeira Angola), contemporary Capoeira, and the techniques of some of the most famous mestres.

3 Training 22

Warming up, basic moves, defense and escape moves, falling, stretching, kicks, training combinations, strengthening exercises, ground movements, and more advanced acrobatic movements.

4 The Music 108

The importance of music in Capoeira, the significance of the bateria, and the instruments that are used.

5 The Game 116

The roda and the jogo. Hierarchy within Capoeira, mestres, and the grading system.

Glossary   124
Making contact   126
Index   128

INTRODUCTION

I began studying Capoeira with my father in Brazil at the tender age of four, and 22 years later I am still hooked. Today, Capoeira is played all over the world, and I often stop to reflect on what attracts people to this art. Since moving to London in 2000, I have taught many students from all walks of life, and have traveled throughout Europe and the USA to share my passion. It is through my teaching that I have fully understood the appeal of Capoeira. People ask me why I practice it when I can never win a "game," and I tell them that Capoeira offers much more than simply scoring points. I have seen Capoeira transform people's lives; it takes them on a journey of self-development, giving them an outlet to express their individuality within the traditional framework of a martial art.

In the following pages I will outline the extraordinary history of Capoeira, from its African roots to the present day. I will also outline its development, and introduce you to its most famous mestres, Mestre Bimba and Mestre Pastinha. Music is vital within Capoeira, but confuses many who are new to the art, so I have included a section on the music and culture of Capoeira, as well as an introduction to the instruments I play. As a beginner, the rules and etiquette of Capoeira may seem alien, so I have included a section on the roda (the circle within which Capoeira is played) and the hierarchy within Capoeira. I also explain the nature of the jogo ("the game"), what it entails, and how it is played. With the help of my students from the Cordão de Ouro school in London, I have broken down some of the basic moves, from the fundamental ginga, kicks, ground movements, and sequences to simple acrobatics. I also include a brief insight into some of the more advanced moves to inspire your progress.

It would be impossible for me to cover all the possible moves within Capoeira, as these often differ from group to group. Capoeira is always growing and developing, and due to the spontaneous nature of the game, new moves are developed all the time. This book is simply a guide for those wishing to explore the world of Capoeira, and I hope that it will inspire you to find a class in your area. As an instructor I can teach students the moves, the music, and the tradition, but it is only by playing the game of Capoeira that you can truly express your individuality. Each Capoeirista will find his or her own game, and this is what makes it such a unique art. Due to the expressive nature of the art, no two schools are exactly the same, and there can sometimes be disagreements over the way things are done. I have simply shared the knowledge, experience, and tradition I have been lucky enough to accumulate within Cordão de Ouro over the last 22 years. I have aimed to be true to the spirit of Capoeira, and I hope that this book inspires you. In the words of Mestre Bimba, one of the founders of modern Capoeira, "Take what I teach you and develop it into your own reality."

Mestre Poncianinho (Ponciano Almeida)

STREET DEMONSTRATIONS OF CAPOEIRA ARE INCREASINGLY COMMON.

opposite MESTRE PONCIANINHO (LEFT) CATCHES CONTRA-MESTRE CASQUINHA WITH AN ACROBATIC KICK CHARACTERISTIC OF CAPOEIRA.

What is Capoeira?

So what is Capoeira? I am often asked to describe Capoeira, to clarify the confusion between whether or not it is a dance or a martial art. Is it a martial art for self-defense, or a dance created for street performance? I will answer that it is neither, but rather a unique art that can be seen as a dance that simulates a fight, or a fight that simulates a dance. Capoeira is an expressive art and difficult to pigeonhole, as it encompasses music, fighting, and fluid movements akin to a dance. A common misconception about Capoeira is that it is a non-contact sport, and some argue that it cannot therefore be a martial art. Contact does not feature heavily in Capoeira and this does, indeed, distinguish it from other forms of martial arts.

Each Capoeirista develops his or her own style of play, with many choosing to avoid contact altogether. A Capoeirista can choose to make contact if there is a failure in their opponent's defense, but as Capoeira does not place an emphasis on rules and point-scoring, contact is not an obligatory part of the game. The way the game is played in Capoeira—the interaction between the Capoeiristas—is considered to be more important than the contact made. You do not win a game of Capoeira by making contact with your opponent, and this is what makes it unique. It should not be forgotten, however, that Capoeira was developed as a fighting art too, and can be used effectively as a form of self-defense. Some of the kicks within Capoeira can be lethal.

Why Capoeira?

The benefits of Capoeira are endless. Not only does it improve your physical strength, flexibility, and reflexes, it also improves your musicality, and encompasses a rich cultural and historical heritage. Many students of Capoeira learn simple Portuguese, and others take the opportunity to visit Brazil as part of their training. Capoeira is a martial art that embraces music, acrobatics, fighting, sport, and philosophy. It is steeped in tradition and ritual, and works to develop the individual on both physical and mental levels.

In Capoeira, you do not train alone, and the social aspect of Capoeira is one of the most appealing features of the art. Capoeira transcends all social boundaries, and in Brazil, for example, you will find Capoeira academies everywhere, from exclusive gyms to favelas (shanty towns). Capoeira is a democratic art, and all Capoeiristas can play together within the roda, regardless of level or ability. The spirit of Capoeira can be extremely playful, and does not rely on physical strength. This enables men, women, and children to train and play together regardless of ability. Capoeira can accommodate both a fierce and awe-inspiring "game" between two strong adults, or a playful exchange between father and son. Capoeira has a place for everyone who is willing to learn.

DESPITE ITS AFRICAN ROOTS, CAPOEIRA IS A BRAZILIAN MARTIAL ART.

MESTRE JOÃO PEQUENO (LEFT) AND MESTRE PAPO AMARELO, TWO WISE MASTERS OF CAPOEIRA ANGOLA ENGAGED IN A BEAUTIFUL GAME.

The history of Capoeira

Although Capoeira is a Brazilian martial art, it does not originate with the Tupi people native to Brazil, but instead has its roots firmly in African culture. There is no question about the African roots of the art, but there is much debate about whether or not it was imported wholesale to Brazil, or developed within the senzalas (the slaves' quarters) on Brazilian soil. The argument tends to favor the theory that Capoeira was developed by African slaves within Brazil, and not brought with them as part of the cultural heritage of their homelands. This is supported by the fact that the history of Capoeira can only be linked to Brazil despite the broad distribution of African slaves worldwide. The history of Capoeira, therefore, begins with the history of African slavery in Brazil.

The colonization of Brazil began in 1500 when a Portuguese fleet chanced upon her shores. The leader of the fleet, Pedro Alves Cabral, promptly declared Brazil to be the possession of the king of Portugal, and for the next three centuries, Brazil remained under Portuguese control. Brazil was colonized and exploited for economic gain, resulting in a need for an extensive labor force. Between 1540 and 1800 Brazil received in excess of two million slaves, who provided labor for the coffee and sugar plantations. The first few hundred years of slavery within Brazil are poorly documented, but what is certain is that the slaves faced cruel and intolerable treatment. What is incredible is that in the face of such adversity and oppression, the African slaves continued to maintain a strong level of cultural identity. Even though their native songs and dances were banned by the slave owners, they still managed to keep their own traditions alive. Capoeira, therefore, was born under the shadow of oppression, and can be seen to represent the triumph of spirit over adversity.

The origins of the word "Capoeira" have also led to much debate, and several theories exist to account for how it got its name. Many believe that the word Capoeira comes from the Tupi language and is derived from the name given to an area of jungle that has been cleared to make way for quilombos (an area of safety and hiding for fugitive slaves). The Tupi words "caa" meaning "down" and "little," and "puoera" meaning "grass," are combined to create a word that quite literally means "hiding in the grass." This explanation gives credence to the underground and hidden practice of Capoeira by the early African slaves.

Another explanation for the use of the word Capoeira is that it is closely related to the word "capa." A capa was a basket carried by African slaves to take birds to the market. A "capoeira" literally refers to the person who bears the basket. It was at the market that games of Capoeira were played, so this explanation also carries much weight. The third theory is that Capoeira finds its roots in the word "kipura," which means "to flutter," and is often used to describe the movements a rooster makes when he fights.

It is often said that Capoeira was developed as a form of self-defense against brutal slave masters. The musical elements are said to have been added to fool the masters into believing that the slaves were simply dancing. Evidence suggests that this account is a myth because even dancing was a forbidden practice. It can also be argued that Capoeira was no match for the guns, knives, and chains used by the oppressors, and would not have been an effective form of self-defense. Capoeira, in effect, was an expression of African culture during a time when it faced the most oppression. Despite this suppression, Capoeira continued to flourish as an underground movement, involving secret meeting places and initiation ceremonies throughout the colonial years.

The development

In 1888, the Golden Law was passed, and slavery was officially abolished in Brazil. In effect, many slaves were made homeless by this and, gaining no financial assistance from the government, were forced to head to the cities in search of work. Competing for work in such a prejudiced society often proved difficult for the slaves, and many turned to petty crime for survival. It was during this period that Capoeira gained its bad reputation and became associated with the criminal classes and anti-government movements. The name Capoeira became synonymous with the bandit, the thief, and the vagrant. Eventually, Capoeira was banned, and a Capoeirista could face the harsh punishment of having his or her tendons cut if caught playing it. Just as it had survived slavery, Capoeira continued to thrive as an outlawed practice. Capoeiristas assumed "apelidos" (nicknames) to avoid detection from the police. This custom is still used today when Capoeiristas assume a Capoeira nickname at their first "batizado" (baptism or grading ceremony). This is another example of how the traditions of Capoeira derive from its ability to resist oppression.

By the twentieth century Capoeira was widespread in Brazil, but still maintained its reputation as the art of the mercenary and thief. Public opinion frowned on it and Capoeira was driven further underground. The suppression did not abate until the 1930s, when Getulio Vargas came to power. Vargas was eager to support all forms of Brazilian cultural expression, including Capoeira. The tide was finally turning in favor of the art. It was during this time that Mestre Bimba (one of the forefathers of modern Capoeira) was invited by the state governor-general to perform an exhibition of his Capoeira Regional for foreign dignitaries. Slowly Capoeira began to move away from its criminal past and toward the respectability of a martial art.

It was during the 1930s that the foundations were laid for modern Capoeira. With the permission of Getulio Vargas, Mestre Bimba opened the doors of the first Capoeira school in 1932, moving Capoeira on to a new level of organization and respectability. Mestre Bimba aimed to promote and teach Capoeira as a form of self-defense, and as a disciplined martial art. He wanted to reclaim the art and free it from its criminal past. The style he developed is referred to as Capoeira Regional and is still practiced as part of contemporary Capoeira. A few years later, Mestre Pastinha opened an

AN EXAMPLE OF A CREATIVE ADVANCED ESCAPE BY MESTRE PONCIANINHO (IN THE AIR).

academy teaching Capoeira Angola in an effort to preserve what he saw as the traditional aspects of the game, and thus the two main styles of Capoeira training were in place. Capoeira moved from being simply a spontaneous, expressive art to becoming a structured and disciplined martial art. During the 1960s and 1970s Capoeira became so structured that it was almost unrecognizable. The traditional style of Capoeira Angola began to decline, and Capoeira saw the emergence of competitions with rules and belt systems inspired by the Asian martial arts.

The history of Capoeira is still evolving. Since the 1970s, Capoeira has spread throughout Brazil and to the rest of the world. Mestres have traveled abroad and academies have opened in Europe and the USA. Despite these developments, Capoeiristas still play using the styles established by Mestre Bimba and Mestre Pastinha during the 1930s. The durability of Capoeira, its adaptability, and resilience are its history. Capoeira was born from slavery, and has survived both oppression and globalization, enabling it to become one of the fastest-growing martial arts in the world.

DEVELOPMENT

The development of contemporary Capoeira is largely indebted to the work of Mestre Bimba and Mestre Pastinha in Brazil during the 1930s. Through their work, two major styles of Capoeira emerged, which are still practiced within Capoeira today. Capoeira Angola is considered to be the purer form of Capoeira, having moved less from the African roots of the game. Capoeira Angola places less emphasis on acrobatic moves and high kicks, instead focusing more on "malandragem," the guile and cunning of the game. It is considered to be a slower game than Regional, and is played close to the ground. Developed by Mestre Bimba, Capoeira Regional is more widely practiced in contemporary Capoeira, and is seen to place more emphasis on harder, faster moves. In contemporary Capoeira, it is vital that you have an understanding of these two distinctive styles.

Mestre Bimba and Capoeira Regional

In 1899, Manoel Dos Reis Machado was born in Salvador, Bahia. He is more commonly known as Mestre Bimba, (Bimba being a nickname given to him by his mother when he was a child). He began to take informal lessons in Capoeira when he was 12 years old under the instruction of an African by the name of Bentinho. Bimba dedicated the rest of his life to Capoeira, developing a style that he called "the Regional fight from Bahia." This style and tradition is now referred to as Capoeira Regional and is practiced worldwide.

When Mestre Bimba first began to practice Capoeira it still had the reputation of being an art used by thieves and vagrants. Practiced in the street or in workplaces, it had no organized structure and was not really considered to be a serious martial art. During the 1930s, however, Mestre Bimba set out to change this, and in 1932 he opened the first Capoeira academy. Mestre Bimba aimed to instill discipline into his students; vagrants were banned from attending classes and anyone arriving late to class was fined. Mestre Bimba famously displayed the rules of his academy on a notice board:

The nine commandments of Mestre Bimba

- Stop smoking. Smoking during training is forbidden.
- Stop drinking. Drinking affects the muscles.
- Do not use Capoeira to impress your friends. Always remember that surprise is your best friend in a fight.
- Do not talk during training. Use the time you are paying for to observe others.
- Always use the ginga.
- Practice the basic exercises daily.
- Don't be scared to get close to your opponent. You will learn more from closer play.
- Eliminate unnecessary tension from your body.
- You're better off being beaten in the roda than in the streets.

Mestre Bimba was an eccentric character, and the first time a student attended his academy, the student was expected to undergo one of Bimba's infamous tests. Potential students were subjected to a test of physical ability, which involved being held in a neck lock by Mestre Bimba without uttering a word of complaint. On the second visit, he would hold their hand and teach them the ginga (see section five, pages 34-35). He

opposite MESTRE PONCIANINHO DEMONSTRATES A "TESOURA" (SCISSORS TAKE-DOWN) WITH IMPRESSIVE PRECISION.

CAPOEIRA AT ITS BEST DEMONSTRATES ELEGANCE, STYLE, AND BALANCE.

believed that the ginga was of fundamental importance within Capoeira, and that without its characteristic sway there was no Capoeira. Mestre Bimba had a hard and disciplined training style, using various techniques to toughen up his students; part of his training involved throwing stones at his students to improve their reflexes. Students were trained to fight with conviction, and to leave their fear at the door. Mestre Bimba himself was a tough fighter, and was often described as "Bimba e bamba" ("Bimba is tough").

Part of the process of formalizing Capoeira was the distinction made between the beginner and the graduate. Before Mestre Bimba's era, students would pick up the moves by watching other Capoeiristas play in the street. Mestre Bimba introduced a training system that involved eight sequences of attack and defense ("sequências"), and beginners were expected to perfect these before they could enter the roda. They were also expected to learn the ginga, the fundamental basic move of Capoeira. They would go on to learn sweeping kicks and the "cintura desprezada" (a sequence of flips culminating in the Capoeirista landing on his or her feet).

Mestre Bimba was an adept of Batuque (a now-extinct African game that involved players attempting to knock each other down with sweeps), and Regional Capoeira's standing sweeps are formidable. He was a competitive man who wanted Capoeira to rank alongside the Asian martial arts that were being introduced into Brazil at the time. He also introduced Capoeira to the world of organized fighting, challenging other martial artists to bouts in the ring. In order to be effective against other martial arts, he introduced grappling techniques, and came under heavy criticism for changing some of the fundamental nature of Capoeira. Mestre Bimba knew that Capoeira would have to change. He must either adapt Capoeira to the rules of the ring or move away from it, finding a new place for Capoeira that fused tradition with the fight.

Although Mestre Bimba faced criticism from some for Westernizing the art, he is largely respected for helping to bring Capoeira into the modern era. By formalizing the training process, and introducing uniforms and rules of conduct, he contributed to the improved image of Capoeira as an art form. Capoeira not only shed its shady image, but began to stand alongside other martial arts as a serious discipline. Although tradition was important to Mestre Bimba, he knew that by emphasizing the fighting aspect of Capoeira he would open it up to a broader audience who would not automatically relate to the traditional elements that were based in African culture. He did continue to use the music traditional to Capoeira, but removed the atabaque (drum) from the bateria (orchestra) due to its connection with candonble (the religion he practiced). Mestre Bimba moved Capoeira into the modern era while retaining many of the traditional elements of the art. Without this modernization, it is difficult to say whether or not Capoeira would have survived.

Mestre Bimba continued to practice Capoeira until his death in 1974. Even in old age, when his limbs were bent and covered in varicose veins, he could kick a younger, fitter man out of the roda. He was a strong, unbending character who moved away from his hometown of Bahia shortly before his death, feeling that the authorities had not given Capoeira the recognition it deserved. He died alone and penniless, away from the students who loved him, and left express wishes that he should not be buried in Bahia. Throughout Brazil, academies closed their doors for seven days as a mark of respect. The respect for Mestre Bimba within the world of Capoeira continues to this day.

Mestre Pastinha and Capoeira Angola

Born in Salvador, Bahia in 1889, Vicente Ferreira Pastinha is most commonly known for preserving the style of Capoeira Angola. He was small and slight from birth, and was bullied as a child. He was taken under the wing of an African named Benedito, who taught him Capoeira as a method of self-defense. Although he continued to have a slight build, Mestre Pastinha held his own against tough men, gaining a job as a bouncer in a local casino. He was also known to carry a sickle, which could be attached to his berimbau (a musical instrument), enabling it to become an offensive weapon for street fighting. Although he used Capoeira as a fighting art to defend himself on the streets, Mestre Pastinha was not simply a fighting man. He is more commonly known as the philosopher and story-teller of Capoeira, who dedicated his life to the love of the art. He loved to analyze Capoeira, to muse on its meanings and moves, and was the first popular Capoeirista to write a book on the subject.

Although many Capoeira Mestres respected the work of Mestre Bimba, others were opposed to the extent to which Capoeira had been modernized. Many resisted the changes made, and looked back to the origins of Capoeira and its African roots. Mestre Pastinha opened his academy a few years after Mestre Bimba, and sought to teach what he believed to be a purer form of Capoeira. This form of Capoeira became known as "Capoeira Angola." The name Angola makes reference to the African slaves who first practiced the art, many of whom originated from Angola.

Like Mestre Bimba, Mestre Pastinha saw Capoeira as a discipline, and tried to distinguish it from the violent forms of Capoeira practiced on the street. He also wanted to improve the image of Capoeira, and by moving it away from the streets and in to the academy, he could provide some discipline. By adding a level of hierarchy and structure, he aimed to stop the use of violent and uncontrolled conduct. He placed great emphasis on the role of the mestre within the roda, believing that it was his duty to keep control. He also believed that his role as mestre gave him the responsibility to ensure that the traditions were continued. He aimed to keep Capoeira pure. Moves from other martial arts were banned, as were high kicks and any form of grappling. He also placed much emphasis on the music of Capoeira, composing many of his own rhythms and songs. Mestre Pastinha recognized the beauty and elegance the music added to the art, and even today you will not see Capoeira Angola played without the music. Mestre Pastinha also introduced uniforms to his academy. The colors black and yellow were taken from his favorite football team, Ipiranga, and are still used by many Angoleiros today.

Mestre Pastinha understood the fighting nature of Capoeira, but firmly believed that it could never be purely competitive. He placed much emphasis on the process and nature of the game, and not on winning and losing. He promoted fair play, manners, and loyalty, placing great emphasis on the "jogo de dentro" (the "inner game"). The inner game is essential to Capoeira Angola, since it demonstrates the student's guile, cunning, and inner strength. Mestre Pastinha took a holistic approach to Capoeira, believing that a student's development should be more than just physical. He acknowledged the psychological and spiritual aspects of Capoeira, and believed that it could be of great benefit to all. He is most famously quoted as saying: "Capoeira is for men, women, and children. The only ones who don't learn Capoeira are those who don't wish to."

Mestre Pastinha's approach to Capoeira attracted the attention of intellectuals and artists, many of whom became his friends. These connections helped him to open a school in a colonial building, establishing himself as the principal Angoleiro of his day. So successful was Mestre Pastinha's Capoeira Angola that in the 1960s, tourists visited his academy to witness displays of "authentic Capoeira." In the 1970s, however, his fortunes took a turn for the worse. His academy was repossessed by the Foundation for Artistic and Cultural Heritage, and was never returned. He lost all of his possessions, and even though he opened another academy, it never matched the scale and prestige of his former years. He eventually lost his eyesight and died penniless in an institution for the elderly. Like Mestre Bimba, he felt let down by the authorities.

It was assumed that after his death, Capoeira Angola would fade into obscurity, seen simply as a dying art for old men, and would be eclipsed by the more dynamic style of Regional. With the growing success of the Regional schools in Rio, it appeared that Angola had seen better days, and that the traditions it embraced were being pushed aside. During the 1980s, however, there was a renewed interest in Afro-Brazilian culture, leading to an increased interest in Capoeira Angola. The Angola style was perceived to be a purer form of Capoeira, and thought to embody more of the

CAPOEIRA IS GROWING RAPIDLY IN POPULARITY. IT IS TAUGHT IN GYMS, DANCE STUDIOS, UNIVERSITIES, AND SCHOOLS AROUND THE WORLD.

traditions passed down from its African originators. In order to revive the dying art, the Grupo de Capoeira Angola Pelourinho was formed. This group called old Capoeira Angola mestres out of obscurity to train with them and, in defiance of the faster, acrobatic forms of the art, encouraged younger men to practice Capoeira Angola. It ceased to be an old man's game, with younger Capoeiristas, such as Mestre Cobra Mansa, proving that it could be just as efficient a fighting technique as the Regional style.

Cordão de Ouro

Since Mestre Bimba and Mestre Pastinha opened their respective academies in the 1930s, countless groups have developed throughout the world. Among these is the school I belong to, called Cordão de Ouro ("Golden Belt"). Cordão de Ouro was formed in 1967 by Mestre

Brasilia and Grand Mestre Suassuna. Mestre Reinaldo Ramos Suassuna was born in Itabuna, Bahia in 1942. He began Capoeira following doctor's orders to improve the health of his joints. He was not a natural Capoeirista and found the ginga difficult to master. After years of dedicated training he became a mestre in Capoeira, and developed a new style called Miudinho. He felt that there was something missing in Capoeira, that the game lacked a closeness, and that Capoeiristas were playing too far away from each other. When he watched the games of mestres such as Mestre Joao Grande and Mestre Joao Pequeno, who played the jogo de dentro, he feared the style would be lost to younger generations. He developed the Miudinho style in order to revive the inner game, common in Capoeira Angola. The word "miudinho" quite literally means "smaller," and Mestre Suassuna could often be heard instructing his students to "play smaller" and "get closer." Many of his training techniques were developed to help his students play together more closely. He would place a berimbau (a monochordic musical instrument) across two chairs and ask his students to play Capoeira underneath it, almost in limbo fashion. They had no choice but to play a lower game. Mestre Suassuna admired the expressive moves of the old Capoeiristas and developed ways of training students in the expressive aspect of Capoeira. He added ornamental aspects to the ginga, making it more dance-like, and encouraged students to mimic animals in order to find new ways of expression within their game. Mestre Suassuna also composed variations of the "toques" (rhythms) played on the berimbau. One toque instructed the players to bring the level of the game up, and to use higher movements. Another toque was used to call the players back to the foot of the berimbau if a game was not proceeding well. Mestre Suassuna was conscious of the need to appeal to young people, so he created challenging moves such as back bends and twists. He incorporated these moves into the game so that they were not simply an exhibition of acrobatics. Through the hard work and dedication of its founding members, Cordão de Ouro went on to become one of the most successful schools in São Paulo.

A family affair

My own mestre is my father, Jose Antonio dos Santos de Almeida, a student of Mestre Suassuna. He was born in Brazil in 1958 and is mestre of Cordão de Ouro in my home town of Guaratinguetá, São Paulo. He has been teaching Capoeira for 25 years. Through Capoeira he also works with homeless children, helping to improve the quality of their lives. Mestre Antonio supervises Cordão de Ouro in London (where I am currently mestre under the name of Poncianinho—"Little Ponciano") and he visits London several times a year in order to teach workshops and to supervise "batizados" (grading ceremonies). I was born in Guaratinguetá in 1980, and began playing Capoeira at just four years old. I took to it like a duck to water, and by the age of 15 I was teaching within the group. Cordão de Ouro respects

A YOUNG PONCIANO SHOWS THAT EXCELLENT FLEXIBILITY IS VITAL.

and values the traditions and styles of the past, and we seek to study and preserve the roots of both Capoeira Angola and Capoeira Regional.

Contemporary Capoeira

In 1972 Capoeira was recognized in Brazil as an official sport, and by the 1980s it had spread from Bahia, Rio de Janeiro, and São Paulo to the whole of Brazil. By the 1990s Capoeira was taught all over the world, and was represented in every state in the USA. Several million people play Capoeira worldwide. Capoeiristas come from all ethnic backgrounds, socio-economic groups, and genders, and women make up a substantial number of students, fulfilling Mestre Pastinha's wish that Capoeira was for all who were willing to learn.

Contemporary Capoeira is no longer split into Angola and Regional styles, since many groups using elements from both styles to teach their students. Although there are core moves and traditions within Capoeira, the style can vary from group to group, making contemporary Capoeira a rich and varied art.

WITH THE RIGHT ATTITUDE AND THE RIGHT TEACHER, CAPOEIRA STUDENTS CAN DEVELOP FANTASTIC SKILLS IN JUST A FEW YEARS.

TRAINING

It is very important to take a serious approach during training to ensure safety. Your spatial awareness will improve in time, but it is important to try to be aware of the existence of others around you. Capoeira is a very safe sport, but you should be aware that most accidents happen while training, and not while playing or fighting. Accidents and injuries tend to happen when students are not aware of the speed and the correct position of the foot while kicking, or are not paying due attention while attacking. Extra care must be taken when practicing spinning kicks, the aú (cartwheel), and other tumbling movements.

Approach to training

Positive thinking is essential during training, as you will not perform well in every class, often finding the movements and correct technique difficult to master. Persistence is the key. Never allow your frustration to get the better of you. For the more experienced Capoeirista there are different phases in your Capoeira training, and you may face times where you feel that you are making slow or very minimal progress, whether in your technique or in your game. There are many challenges within Capoeira with so many things to learn. When you get to a certain level you will notice more movements within the game, but you may not have reached the level of flexibility or strength to reproduce these movements. At this stage you might begin to put more pressure on yourself and have higher expectations, but it is better to have a clear understanding of the moves and approach them step by step. Each mestre will have his or her own way of teaching, and systems within each group may vary. By paying close attention to your particular mestre, your game will improve immensely. It is also important to share the knowledge you gain within Capoeira, as this will develop your future ability to teach, and to clarify in your own mind the moves your body makes. A student that never shares may become an egotistical Capoeirista who will never reach his full potential.

No one approach will enable you to achieve your goals, as Capoeira is a holistic art. I believe that only a combination of elements can lead to progress, and my mestre taught me three basic rules of training:

Three basic rules of training

- Quality in the technique and an appropriate amount of training.
- Good nutrition.
- Rest.

Combining an appropriate number of training hours with a balanced diet, and sufficient rest will make a considerable difference to your performance.

The mind will also play an important role in your performance, skill, and ability to succeed in Capoeira. Capoeira can help you to be a more positive and energetic person, but you must be strong at difficult moments and show strength of character. The way you live your life outside of the class, in your daily life, and on the streets, will reflect in your game. Be aware of your fears and insecurities, and be careful that they don't transform into submission or aggression. Capoeira is the art of being able to fight with a smile on your face.

opposite MANY FACTORS COMBINE TO MAKE A GOOD CAPOEIRISTA, BUT GOOD NUTRITION, REST, AND TRAINING ARE THE BASICS.

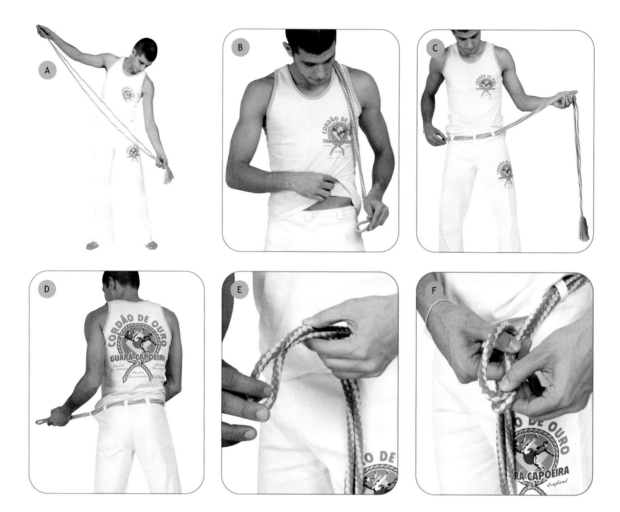

How to tie the Capoeira belt

The Capoeira belt is called the "cordão" (cord). Some groups may call their belt the "corda" (rope), depending on how it is made. There are a few different types of belts in Capoeira, and the Capoeira cordão differs from belts in other martial arts because it is a cord shape and not flat. The cordão is made from wool and is woven with the color, or colors, of the grade. The corda is a rope that is dyed to the color of each grade. My own group, Cordão de Ouro, uses cordãos that are woven in the traditional way by the students of the academy in the lead-up to the batizado. The weaving of the belts is time-consuming, so some groups buy the belts pre-woven. All of the belts for my London group are hand-woven by students of my father's academy in Brazil.

A   Double up your belt, making sure the ends are at equal lengths.

B   Feed the middle part of your belt through the first belt loop to the left of your Capoeira trousers.

C   Take the belt through the first three belt loops.

D   Continue to feed the belt through all of the belt loops.

E   Once your belt has been fed through the last belt loop and is back around to your left side, take the end of the belt in your right hand.

F   Fold the belt back and put your fingers through the loop to hold the lower part of the belt, which you can see through the loop that has just been made.

G   Pull the doubled-up part of the belt you have just taken with your right hand, and take it through the top end of the belt that you had first folded back, in order to create a new loop. Hold the new loop in your left hand.

H   Take hold of the other end of the belt, holding the loop open with your right hand.

I   Feed the ends of your belt through the loop, and pull it through.

J   Pull the end of your belt tight.

K   A correctly tied belt will stay tied while you are practicing and playing Capoeira, and will also be easy to untie.

Uniforms

Most groups wear white uniforms consisting of trousers and a t-shirt or vest. The white uniform comes from an old tradition where the Capoeiristas would play wearing white suits; a highly skilled player would emerge from the game with an unmarked suit. The group logo is normally emblazoned on the front of the uniform. Capoeira trousers are made of fabric that stretches to allow maximum movement.

Warming up

The warm-up is the first part of any Capoeira class and should be taken as seriously as the actual learning of the movements. The warm-up raises the body temperature and improves the oxygen supply to the muscles. This stimulates blood sugar and adrenaline levels, preparing the body for action. The preparation of the heart muscle for rigorous exercise is particularly important to individuals who may have cardiovascular problems. Warming up reduces the workload on the cardiac muscle, and helps to provide it with an adequate blood supply. Always talk to your doctor, though, before beginning any exercise regime. The warm-up also prepares your body for the stress of activity and will help to improve your performance. It also helps to prevent or reduce muscle soreness, strains, and the tearing of muscle fibres or tendons.

The basic moves of Capoeira can also be used in the warm-up section. It is very important for your joints to be warmed up thoroughly to prepare your body for the impact of kicks, falls, and the hyper-extended movements that it will endure. A Capoeira warm-up begins with small movements to mobilize your joints. These will be incorporated into base moves such as the ginga and cocorinha to a relatively slow rhythm, and will usually run straight through to the first part of your technical training. A safe and efficient warm-up should have a gradual progression of intensity and last no less than ten minutes. It is always a good idea for you to arrive early and find a space for you to start warming up before the class; in this way you will gain more from your training sessions.

Mobilizing the neck and shoulders

A   Start in a relaxed position with your feet shoulder-width apart, and your knees soft.

B–C Look to the left and right over your shoulders, keeping the abdominals firm and the spine long. Repeat this several times.

D–E Maintain the same posture and bring your ear toward your right and left shoulders. Gently stretch the side of your neck and keep the spine long as you go through the central position of the head.

F–G–H Bring your shoulders forward, up toward your ears, and back around in a clockwise motion, creating circular movements with both shoulders.

(Warming up continued)

I   Start from a standing position with your abdominals firm, facing forward.

J   Bring your head and shoulders forward and start to roll down through your spine toward the floor.

K   Roll through your spine all the way down to the floor, and let your upper body hang over.

L   Roll back up through your spine leaving your head relaxed forward.

M   Return to an upright standing position and repeat the exercise several times.

Warming up your wrists

Warming up the wrists is vital in Capoeira. You will need to build up a lot of strength in your wrists, as many of the movements practiced place a lot of body weight on them. Strong wrists play an important role in supporting your body in handstands and enduring the impact of landing from acrobatic moves.

A—B Keep your arms in front of your body and make circular movements with your hands from the wrists. Perform this exercise both clockwise and anti-clockwise, and repeat it both ways several times.

Warming up the knees and hip flexors (front of the hip)

This exercise will help you to find your center and balance at the beginning of the class, as well as helping to warm up the hip area.

A   Start from a standing position and bring your right knee up toward your chest. Hold the knee gently in this position for several seconds.

B   Repeat this exercise with the other leg. Remember to keep your supporting knee straight and your spine long.

C   Start in a wide stance with your knees bent and arms to the side.

D   Swivel your feet and body to the left, keeping your knees bent into a low lunge with your right arm folding in.

E–F Turn back to face the front and repeat this movement on the other side. Repeat all these small gentle movements several times, keeping relaxed and at ease.

Rises

Rises are a gentle way of warming up your calves and are also good for finding your center of balance at the start of the class.

A   Start in a standing position and rise up on to the balls of your feet. Keep the knees straight and start to raise your arms up at the sides.

B   While rising, bring your arms all the way up and over your head. Return to the standing position by reversing the carriage of the arms back down by your sides as you lower your heels. Repeat this several times.

31

Preparatory stretches

Preparatory stretches are small, gentle stretches that should only be held for a few seconds at a time. They are good for releasing tension during the warm-up, before you move on to the more physically demanding section of the class. These stretches should only be attempted at the end of the warm-up section when your muscles are already warm.

Lunge stretch

A   To stretch both the buttocks and the hip flexors, take a long, low lunge position with your back leg straight and your front leg bent by your right side. Keep your fingers pointing toward your back leg to stretch your wrists and the inside of your arms. Repeat this stretch with both legs, keeping it gentle and relaxed.

Inside thigh stretch

A—B   Lunge down to the floor, keeping your left knee pointing to the front, your right leg out to the side and slightly turned out. Place both hands on the floor and lean your upper body slightly forward keeping yourself slightly off the floor. Repeat this stretch on both sides.

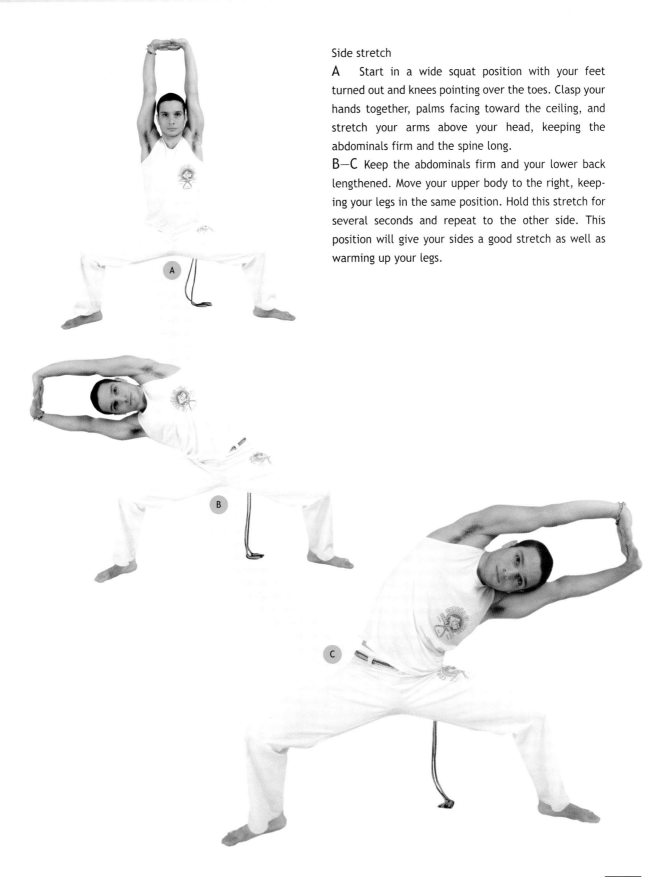

Side stretch

A Start in a wide squat position with your feet turned out and knees pointing over the toes. Clasp your hands together, palms facing toward the ceiling, and stretch your arms above your head, keeping the abdominals firm and the spine long.

B—C Keep the abdominals firm and your lower back lengthened. Move your upper body to the right, keeping your legs in the same position. Hold this stretch for several seconds and repeat to the other side. This position will give your sides a good stretch as well as warming up your legs.

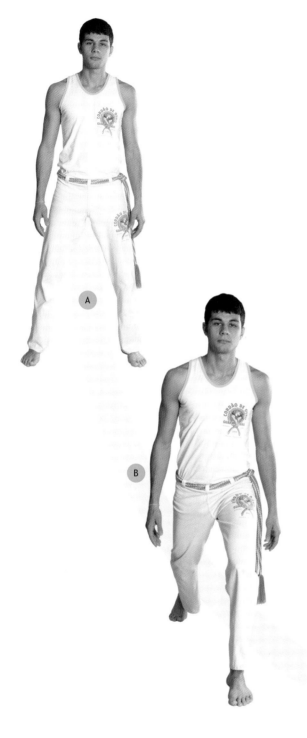

A

B

The ginga

The ginga (pronounced "jinga") is fundamental to Capoeira, and is the first movement you should learn. It is the ginga that creates the natural swing or sway, and combined with the music, makes Capoeira a unique martial art. Its use is vital within Capoeira, as it helps you to develop spatial awareness, and a keen sense of rhythm. Many movements derive from the ginga and it should never be neglected within your game.

The ginga is an important part of your training and you will usually start to ginga as part of your warm-up, gradually incorporating other moves as you progress. You can use the ginga within the game to escape, attack, counter-attack, and confuse your opponent. Your aim is to develop a strong base in your ginga and work toward achieving your own natural swing or sway;

B (SIDE VIEW)

this will help you to develop expression within your game. Each Capoeirista will have his or her own style of ginga, and it is important to try to find your own way of expressing yourself through this basic movement. When you begin to practice with the music, you will start to connect your body to the rhythms that are being played by the bateria, and this will allow you to feel the swing of the ginga.

The ginga will enable you to move around the roda. This is the movement used to change direction within the game, according to the position of your opponent. The speed and style of the ginga will depend on the nature of the game; the ginga may be fast or slow, sharp or smooth.

A Stand with your feet parallel and shoulder-width apart. Look straight ahead, keeping your knees soft, and maintain a strong sense of grounding.

B The ginga starts by taking your right foot back, touching the floor with the ball of your foot. Bring the same foot back to the initial position (picture A) and repeat with the left leg, making a triangle shape on the floor. Repeat with each leg in a continual motion. Note: Your hips must be facing forward the whole time.

C As you take the right leg back, bring the right arm forward and across your chest, leaving the left arm out to the side. Repeat this movement with the left leg and combine them to produce a smooth, simultaneous movement. You will switch the arms as you switch the legs simultaneously.

C

C (SIDE VIEW)

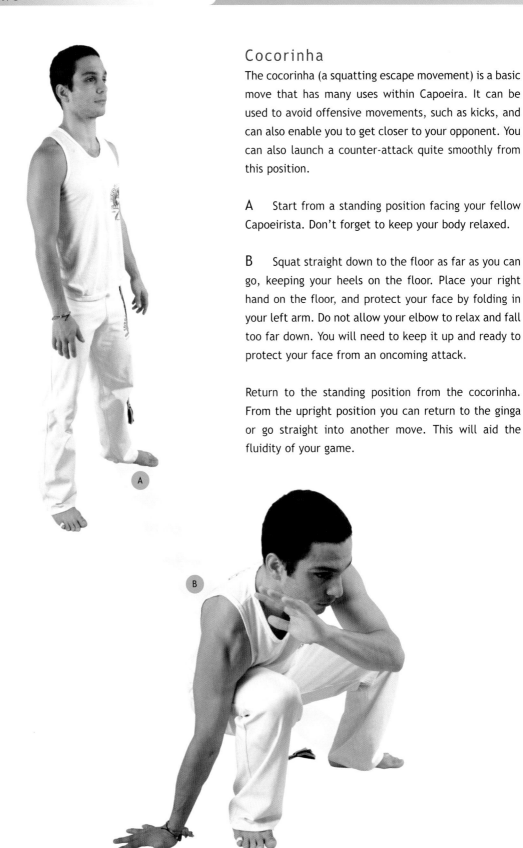

Cocorinha

The cocorinha (a squatting escape movement) is a basic move that has many uses within Capoeira. It can be used to avoid offensive movements, such as kicks, and can also enable you to get closer to your opponent. You can also launch a counter-attack quite smoothly from this position.

A Start from a standing position facing your fellow Capoeirista. Don't forget to keep your body relaxed.

B Squat straight down to the floor as far as you can go, keeping your heels on the floor. Place your right hand on the floor, and protect your face by folding in your left arm. Do not allow your elbow to relax and fall too far down. You will need to keep it up and ready to protect your face from an oncoming attack.

Return to the standing position from the cocorinha. From the upright position you can return to the ginga or go straight into another move. This will aid the fluidity of your game.

Queda de rins

"Queda de rins" quite literally means a "fall onto the kidneys". It's a grounded movement that brings you close to the floor. Your body is lowered on to your elbow, which is locked into the side of your body just around the hip. Queda de rins is another classic Capoeira move that clearly differentiates Capoeira from other martial arts. This movement can be used to defend yourself when the knees are brought in close to your body. The queda de rins technique can also be used during a kick, such as a meia lua de compasso, thus lowering the level of the kick.

The queda de rins increases upper-body strength tremendously, and it will also increase your agility and help you to gain more body control. The use of this technique, once perfected, can be useful in many moves and situations to balance and turn. There are many varieties of fall that stem from the basic queda de rins, and highly skilled movements using it can be found frequently in a game of miudinho. This technique can be used to balance and hold a position, or can be used as a transition from one move to another.

A   We have shown this movement from the back to give you a clear idea of where exactly you need to lock your elbow into the side. Start from a small squat position, facing the front.

B   Shift your body weight to the right by placing your right hand on the floor. Bring your left arm up over your head, and keep your focus forward.

C   Bring the left arm up all the way over your head and place it on the floor. Coming up off of your heels, push your body weight into the right foot.

(Continued)

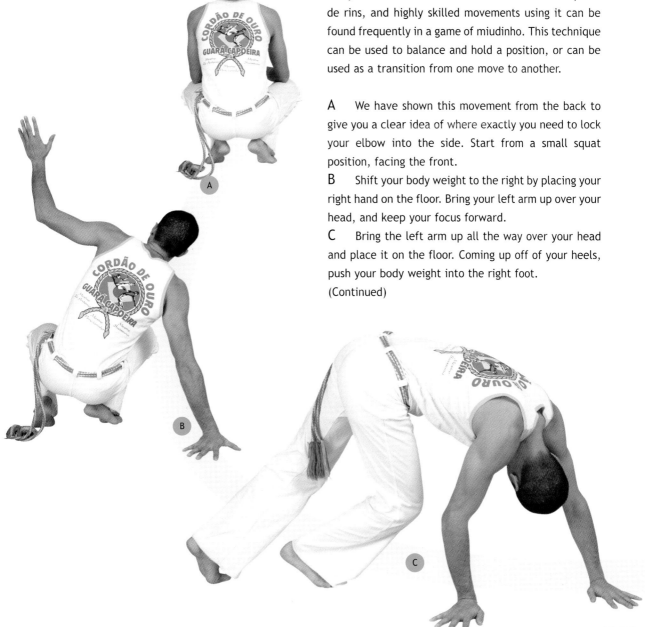

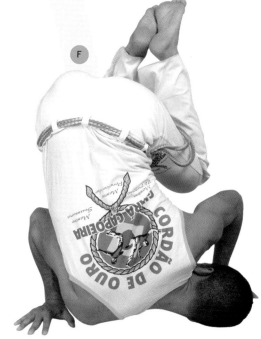

(Continued)

D   Lower your body to the right elbow, with the side of your head resting on the floor and your left arm placed in front of your body for support. In this example the right knee is resting slightly on the floor with the left leg extended out. Normally, the right knee should not touch the floor, but as a beginner you can put your knee on the floor until you are strong enough to maintain the position sufficiently to raise it.

E   Stay in the same position and bring your knees in toward your chest. Notice how your elbow is locked into the left side just above your hip

F   Aim to balance with your elbow locked into your side, and keep your knees tucked in toward your chest. Use your left hand on the floor in front of you to support your balance.

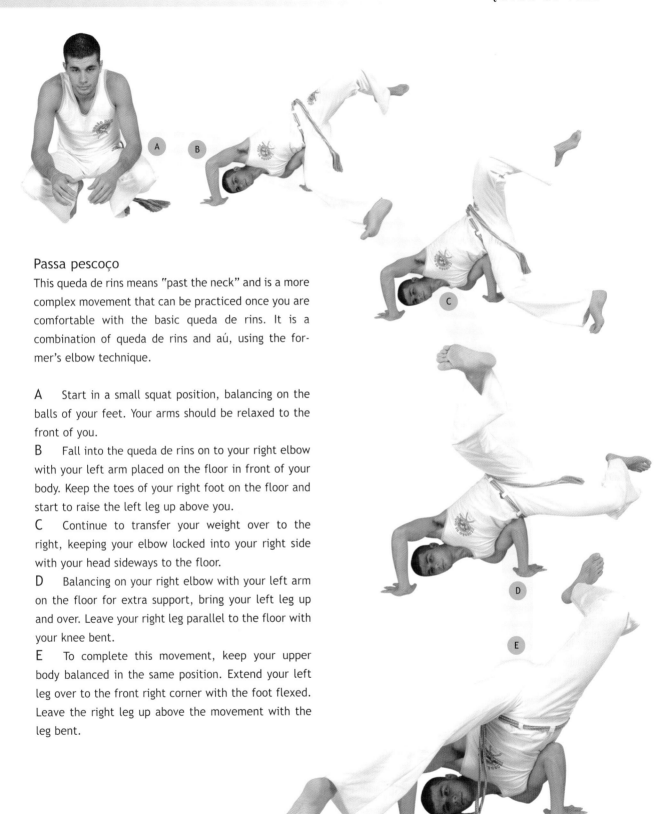

Passa pescoço

This queda de rins means "past the neck" and is a more complex movement that can be practiced once you are comfortable with the basic queda de rins. It is a combination of queda de rins and aú, using the former's elbow technique.

A   Start in a small squat position, balancing on the balls of your feet. Your arms should be relaxed to the front of you.

B   Fall into the queda de rins on to your right elbow with your left arm placed on the floor in front of your body. Keep the toes of your right foot on the floor and start to raise the left leg up above you.

C   Continue to transfer your weight over to the right, keeping your elbow locked into your right side with your head sideways to the floor.

D   Balancing on your right elbow with your left arm on the floor for extra support, bring your left leg up and over. Leave your right leg parallel to the floor with your knee bent.

E   To complete this movement, keep your upper body balanced in the same position. Extend your left leg over to the front right corner with the foot flexed. Leave the right leg up above the movement with the leg bent.

A

B

Defense and escape moves

Resistência

"Resistência" ("to resist") is a classic Capoeira move and an ideal movement for beginners. It will help to strengthen your back, and begin to give you an understanding of arching backward. This movement is also an effective defense movement, and is the root of many advanced escapes. In training for it, you will also improve the flexibility of your lower back.

A   Start from a relaxed standing position.
B   Bring your right arm up and across to protect your face, and allow your left arm to swing back slightly behind your body.
C   As your knees bend, arch your lower back and push your pelvis forward. Your left arm continues to swing back and your right arm comes up higher to protect your face, with the elbow ready to angle itself

higher if it is necessary to protect the face farther.
D   The resistência can go as far back as necessary; however, it is important for you to prevent your head from tilting back, as eye contact needs to be maintained with your fellow Capoeirista.
E   You can practice this move alone to gain strength in the lower back, and also with a fellow Capoeirista to improve your reflexes. This move can be practiced with a few different kicks; here we have used a benção. Notice how the resistência is allowing the Capoeirista to escape the kick while maintaining eye contact. From this position the Capoeirista executing the resistência could attempt to transform the resistência into a disiqulibrante, such as a rasteira, to take his fellow Capoeirista off balance.

A

B

Esquiva

Esquiva is a basic movement that is used to escape from kicks. The term means "to dodge," which is the basic purpose of the movement. There are a few variations of this movement to enable you to adapt your escape, depending on the angle from which an attack is coming, and on the next movement you intend to execute. In order to connect the esquiva to other moves or directions, it is important to know various types of esquivas. The general rule of any type of esquiva is that one leg takes the majority of your body weight, and that you are using your arms correctly to enable you to protect your face and upper body.

Esquiva baixa (low escape)

A Start from the ginga position, and make sure that you have a good solid base with depth. Keep your right arm up to protect your face, and maintain a forward focus.

B Slide your right foot back, allowing the ginga position to become wider and deeper. As you do this your hand reaches for the floor to support your balance, your chest moves toward your left thigh, and your right arm comes up to protect your face. You should feel well-balanced, grounded, and strong in this position. Maintain eye contact all the way through. To return from this movement you can either return to a ginga position, or connect the esquiva baixa to a low floor movement.

C Here the esquiva baixa is being used to escape a meia lua de compasso. The Capoeirista in the esquiva baixa has a good, strong, and balanced base, which will allow her to move to any position that she chooses with ease, whether it be an upright or low move.

C

Esquiva lateral (sideways escape)

A   Start from the ginga position with your right leg back.

B   Step sideways with your right leg so that you move into a lunge position. Your right foot should be turned out and your right knee bent. Your left foot stays parallel with the leg straight, the weight of the body needs to be mainly on your right leg.

C   Lower your chest to your right knee and bring your right arm behind your leg with your hand on the floor. Fold your left arm in to protect your face.

From the esquiva position come straight back up to the ginga position and continue to ginga. You can then repeat this on the other side starting from the ginga position. Repeating this movement to Capoeira music will create a "swing".

To come out of the esquiva baixa you return to a parallel position ready to practice this movement with the other leg. Always practice on both sides, as you never know which side your opponent's attack may come from. In a class situation we would practice this move both alone and with a partner. As a beginner, start slowly with a partner, and very gradually increase the speed. Take care not to anticipate the esquiva before the attack, as the main point of the exercise is to train your reflexes and not simply to practice the move.

Negativa

The direct translation of negativa is "negative," but the actual significance of this word in relation to its purpose would be "to reject"—you would be refusing an attack by allowing it to go over your body. The negativa is a very dynamic movement that enables you to move in different directions, and to escape at the same time. It is a basic movement that teaches you to move on the floor. Many floor movements start from this move; not only can you protect yourself with the negativa, you can also increase the fluidity within your game with the use of this movement. Once you have learned the negativa, try to link it to other moves, such as aú de cabeça, in order to make your game more interesting. There are a few types of negativa that use the same name, but differ in form and purpose.

Negativa 1

This type of negativa can be found in most of Mestre Bimba's Regional-style sequences.

A   Start from the ginga position, with the left foot forward and the right foot back. Your right arm should be up to protect your face, with the left arm down at your left side.

B   Bring the back leg from the ginga position through by swinging your leg forward. Keep your leg turned out, with your foot flexed and your toes pointed forward. At the same time move both arms to your right side over your right leg. Bend the left knee, allowing you to carry yourself to the floor. Your arms need to be well over to enable your hands to land on the floor before any other part of your body touches the ground.

C   As your hands reach the floor, your foot is kept off the ground, and should be flexed with your toes pointing toward the right. Your head is positioned so that your ear is parallel to the floor—this way you can maintain your focus to the front.

D   This is the full negativa position. Notice how the Capoeirista is using her strength to keep her body off the floor. Do not allow your body to collapse, or your leg to rest on the floor. Your arms need to be ready to spring your body back into action. Your right elbow is kept close to your right side, and your left hand should be in a good position, enabling you to support your body comfortably.

E   Here you can see the negativa in action. The Capoeirista has lowered herself down with speed and efficiency to hook her right foot around the base leg of her fellow Capoeirsta's bençáo kick. This enables her to test his balance, if desired.

To return from this full negativa position you can use the following saida (exit).

A   Push your hands into the floor, bringing your body up. Maintain the negativa position, but allow your arms to stretch, and your right foot to rest on the floor.

B   Using your hands and the right foot that has just been placed on the floor, bring your body around and slightly rise on to your right foot, bringing your left heel toward your backside.

C   Place your left foot on to the floor until you are in a lunge position with your hands on the floor, and look through your arms and legs at your partner.

D   Return to an upright position by coming up and swiveling your feet and body around to face your partner in the ginga position, with your right leg back.

Negativa 2

The following negativa is more commonly found in a game of Capoeira Angola. This movement can be executed from a ginga position. It is a low escape, and once well trained, you can move from this position into any other movement with speed and ease for an effective escape. This negativa can also be used as a fall. If your opponent attacks you with a sweep it is an excellent position to fall into, as you can land in a well-balanced position, enabling you to make a quick recovery into another movement.

A   Start in a squat position, with your heels slightly raised off the floor. Your weight should be on the balls of your feet, and you should have a good, balanced position.

B   Move your body to the side. Place both of your hands on the floor to the side of your body. Stretch your left leg out to the side with your right knee pointing forward. Your right heel remains off the floor.

(Continued)

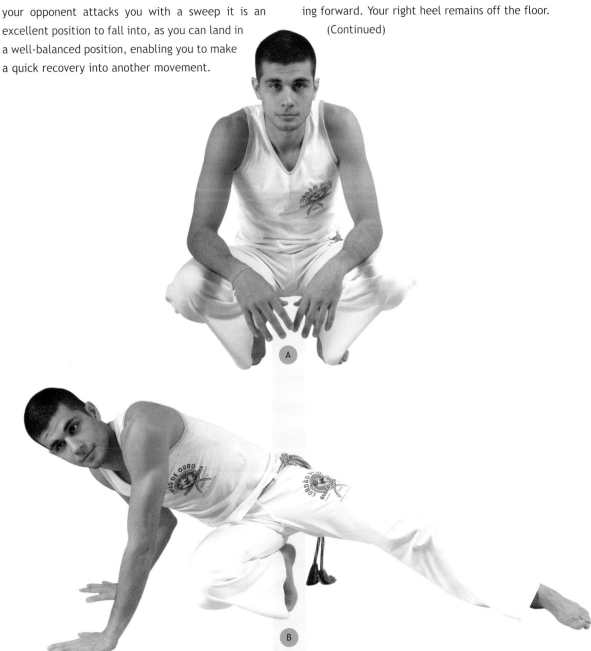

(Continued)

C   Lower your body to the side to the full negativa position. Your head stays parallel to the floor, enabling you to maintain a forward focus, and your right elbow comes in close to the right side of your body. In this position you are taking the full weight of your body on your arms, preventing your body from collapsing on to the floor.

D   To come out of the negativa, push up your body with your arms, keeping the right heel off the floor.

E   Bring your right arm over your head as you swivel your body to the left using your right foot and your left arm. Continue to maintain eye contact with your partner.

F   Continue to swivel your body on your left foot, and place your free hand on the floor. Start to bring your right leg around.

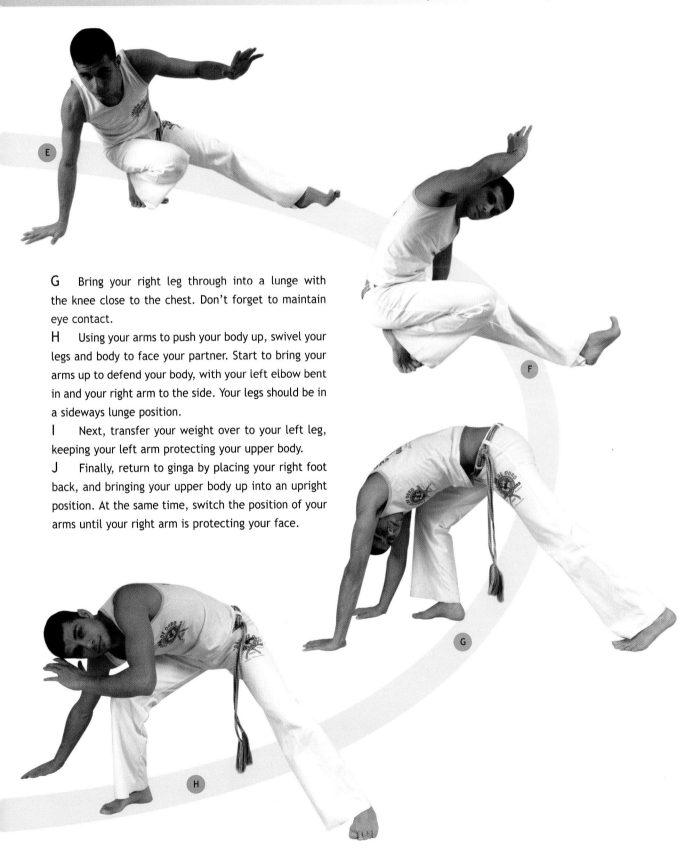

G Bring your right leg through into a lunge with the knee close to the chest. Don't forget to maintain eye contact.

H Using your arms to push your body up, swivel your legs and body to face your partner. Start to bring your arms up to defend your body, with your left elbow bent in and your right arm to the side. Your legs should be in a sideways lunge position.

I Next, transfer your weight over to your left leg, keeping your left arm protecting your upper body.

J Finally, return to ginga by placing your right foot back, and bringing your upper body up into an upright position. At the same time, switch the position of your arms until your right arm is protecting your face.

Negativa recuada

The translation of the word "recuada" means "to go backward." An important aspect of this defense move is that you are moving backward in order to give yourself enough distance to counter-attack. You can use this position to gain momentum for another attack, making this negativa a very dynamic movement.

A   Start from the ginga position, with your right foot forward and your left foot back. Your left arm should be up to protect your face, with your right arm down to your right side.

B   From the ginga position, start to lower yourself down to the floor by transferring the weight of your body on to your back foot. Keep your left arm up protecting your face, and maintain eye contact.

C   Lower yourself fully to the ground, and place your right hand on the floor for support. Your left heel should be off the floor, enabling you to sit on your back heel. Do not collapse into this position, but maintain a good balance. This will ensure that you are able to move easily if and when required.

D   To return from the negativa position, you can come back to ginga. You can reverse the movement by using your right hand to push yourself off the floor.

E   Transferring your weight over the front leg, return to the full ginga position, and continue play.

F   Here is a front view of the negativa. Notice how the Capoeirista has not collapsed on to the back foot, but is supporting his balance and body weight through the back foot with a good, relaxed, supporting right hand.

C

D

F

E

Rolê

Rolê ("roll") is a movement that can be used to escape an attack, and can also be used to move around the roda. Although it's direct translation means "to roll," you are not actually rolling your body on the floor; you are using your arms and feet to move low on the ground in a continuous turning motion, stepping one leg over the other. You can link this move to other moves, making it a connecting transitional movement. It is similar to a negativa, but a negativa that allows you to move across the floor sideways, making this a very useful movement within the game.

A   Start in a low position with your weight balanced on your back right heel. Your left leg should be relaxed to the front, and your left arm placed on the floor supporting your balance. Your focus should be forward with your right arm folded across to protect the face.

B   Pivot on your left leg and step over it with your right leg while you bring your right arm over your head and place it on the floor. Lift your right leg off the floor by bringing your heel in toward the back of your leg. Keep your focus toward your partner.

C   Turn slightly farther around to your left, and place your right leg on to the floor, until you are in a lunge position with your left leg straight. Remember to keep your focus toward your partner.

D   Transfer your weight on to the back foot from the lunge position, and remove your left hand from the floor to fold in toward your chest. Your left leg stays out to the front with a relaxed knee.

E   Shift your weight back to the starting position by moving your arms; the left hand should be placed on the floor supporting the balance, and the right arm folded in to protect your face.

Falling

The following movements will teach you how to fall correctly. It is important to practice these movements in order to begin to feel comfortable with falling on to your hands and feet. A Capoeirista should avoid any part of his body, other than the hands and feet, from touching the floor when he is falling. It is inevitable that while playing and training Capoeira you will fall. The importance of learning how to fall well is crucial in order to avoid injury, and it also enables the Capoeirista to continue his game smoothly. Due to the nature of the game, we try to avoid staying on the floor after a fall, as a Capoeirista needs to be ready immediately to continue the game. There are no mats in Capoeira and you will often find yourself playing on hard surfaces, especially if, as an experienced Capoeirista, you are participating in a street roda. A fall can often lead to another movement; if you recover quickly enough, you can manage to use the fall to spring into another move and the fall can pass unnoticed, bringing your game to another level. There is a famous phrase in the Capoeira world that is very relevant here: "A good Capoeirista doesn't fall, but when he does, he falls well."

These falling techniques are used by everyone, from beginners to the more advanced, but they require practice to enable you to support your body off the floor. To fall well can be considered as skillful as a successful attack within the Capoeira game, and a great fall can become a magical moment within the roda.

Queda de quatro

The "queda de quatro" ("falling on all fours") teaches you how to fall on a strong base and is a very safe way of falling. This is a movement that should never be taken for granted. Although you may appear vulnerable, you are actually in a very safe and strong position.

A   From standing, go through to a squatting position.
B   Fall backward, throwing both arms back behind your body. Prepare your hands to land properly on the floor to avoid landing on your fingers.
C   Land on both your hands at the same time and keep your elbows supple. Do not lock your arms as you land. Using your arms and your feet, keep your body off the floor, holding a forward focus throughout.

Queda de três

"Queda de três" ("falling on three limbs") is mainly used when one leg has been swept away by your opponent, knocking you off balance. As you will have lost your base from the sweep, you need to use everything else you have available to land safely and efficiently.

A   From the standing position, squat and throw yourself to the floor. Swing your right leg forward and both your arms back, preparing your hands for landing.
B   Continue to throw your leg forward as you fall.
C   Land on your hands with your elbows soft, and bring your right leg up to protect your body from attack. Your left knee will remain bent and your focus held forward. Keep your body off the floor and maintain your balance in this position to enable you to shift to another move at ease, without allowing your body to touch the floor. Remember to maintain eye contact with your partner.

B   C

B   C

Stretching to improve flexibility

Flexibility within Capoeira is a great asset, but not everyone is born with natural flexibility; in fact, most people have to work at it. Factors such as gender and age also affect flexibility, with younger women generally being the most flexible. Genetic factors may also play a part in flexibility and different areas of the body will be more flexible than others.

It is important not to be competitive when stretching with others, as we all have our own strengths and weaknesses. In order to increase your flexibility it is vital to follow a good stretching routine and, if followed sensibly, you will notice a gradual, steady improvement in the range of your movements. Patience is vital when following a stretching program as it is better to stretch slowly and correctly than to force the body too quickly, which can cause injury. Stretching reduces the risk of injury to the joints, tendons, and muscles. In order to stretch safely, it is not advisable to attempt stretches when your muscles are cold. Even the most experienced Capoeirista can pull a hamstring if his or her muscles are not prepared. An amazing kick may only take seconds to perform, but if it is done when the muscles are cold, the resulting injury incurred could last months, if not a lifetime.

To prepare for stretching, you can follow both an aerobic and joint rotation warm-up. Joint rotations should encompass the following body parts: wrists, elbows, shoulders, neck, trunk/waist, hips, legs, knees, ankles, fingers, knuckles, and toes. For aerobic exercises, simple and natural movements that do not overstretch your body will warm you up sufficiently. These are especially important in cold weather, or if you are feeling particularly stiff. Fast walking, marching, or gentle jogging should do the trick. Any exercise that increases the pulse rate also raises the core body temperature and this will prepare you to stretch. Most people are more flexible during the afternoon and in warmer environments.

There are different types of stretches, the two most commonly used being static and dynamic. Static stretches should be performed first, as dynamic stretches are the most likely to cause tears in your muscles if you are ill-prepared. A static stretch involves easing the body gently into a stretch and holding it. Dynamic stretches are swings of the arms and legs that gradually push the body beyond its normal range of movements. These can be started at half speed to ease the body into the movement.

Due to intense concentration, many people forget to breathe during stretches. Make sure that you take deep

A

breaths; by exhaling when you go into a stretch you may be able to push the move even farther. It is also detrimental to bounce during a stretch, and stretches should only be held for a maximum of 30 seconds before alternating. Also, don't forget to drink plenty of water as dehydration during exercise can cause the muscles to cramp.

If you are serious about increasing your flexibility, it is advisable to perform a stretching routine every day, although it may be sensible to rest after any extreme activity. It is also important to stretch after Capoeira. These stretches will help you to make the most progress with becoming more flexible. It will also help to reduce the cramping and soreness of muscles the next day, which is caused by lactic acid build-up created by exercise.

Never be tempted to overstretch. It is normal to feel some discomfort like pins and needles, but sharp pains and twinges are a warning sign to stop; always adhere to the signals your body gives you. Never force a stretch; pushing the muscles too far, too quickly will only result in injury and delay the progress of your flexibility considerably. When done sensibly, stretching exercises can be a fun and rewarding part of a warm-up routine, and will improve your range of movements within the game of Capoeira.

Calf, hamstring, and back stretch

A   This stretch is excellent for the calves, hamstrings, and back as it helps to release the tension from the spine. Aim to relax your body as far over your legs as possible, with your head relaxed forward, and reach for your toes with your elbows relaxed down to the floor. You may not be able to fold all the way down at first, but go as far as you can keeping your legs straight and your head relaxed forward.

Deeper combined inner thigh and side stretch

A   Start in a sitting position, with your legs apart, your knees straight, and your body upright. Reach over to your right side by taking your right arm over your head toward your foot as far as you can go; you may need to place your left hand on the floor for support. (Continued)

(Continued)

B   After holding this position come up through the center, and take the side stretch to your left.

C   Return from the side stretch and lower your chest to the floor in the center of your legs. Your aim is to relax your whole upper body on to the floor in front of you. This may take some time to master. Remember, patience is the key.

D   Once you are feeling confident with your upper body relaxed on to the floor, extend your arms out to the front to achieve a deeper stretch in the hips.

The hamstring stretch

A   Place your right leg on your kneeling partner's right shoulder. This is the basic form of the stretch.

B   For a deeper hamstring stretch, get your partner to stand up slowly from the kneeling position. You are aiming to keep both knees straight for maximum stretch. Repeat with the other leg.

Stretching the leg in the martelo position

This stretch will improve line, height, and all-round flexibility in preparation for the martelo and chapa kick.

A   Place your martelo kick on your kneeling partner's shoulder. You should feel this stretch in the inside thigh of the kicking leg.

B   To increase this stretch, your partner stands up while you maintain the martelo position. You should now feel the stretch in both of your inside thighs. This position also works the flexibility of the hips.

Quadriceps stretch

The quadriceps, or thigh muscles, are used extensively for many movements in Capoeira, such as the ginga and cocorinha. It is important to stretch these muscles after a Capoeira class, as you will require flexibility in your thighs.

A   Start from a standing position.

B   Grasp your foot and bring your heel toward your backside. Keep your hips pushed forward and the knees together. While stretching your thigh, push your shoulders down and back to open your chest.

Shoulder stretch

This stretch is excellent for stretching the shoulders while opening out the chest and hips.

A   Start in a low position with your backside raised off the floor.

B   Push your hips toward the ceiling and straighten your arms, pushing your shoulders back.

C   Push your hips farther toward the ceiling, fully straighten your arms, and gently allow your head to relax back.

61

Cabeçada

The "cabeçada" ("head butt") is a very important classic Capoeira attack. It is a raw, dangerous, and delicate movement. A Capoeirista should never underestimate the power of a head butt. Great skill is required to use it, as it can be a vulnerable position for you to be in if you haven't judged your timing and distance correctly. Cabeçada is normally applied on the stomach area, but some techniques aim toward the face, which can obviously be quite nasty. A Capoeirista can be famous for giving a good cabeçada—there are even songs in Capoeira that refer to cabeçeiros (a person who is good at applying the cabeçada). The best cabeçadas always come as a real surprise.

A Capoeiristas (i) and (ii) start in the ginga position. Capoeirista (i) starts with her right leg back, and Capoeirista (ii) mirrors her with his left leg back in the ginga.

B Capoeirista (i) attacks Capoeirista (ii) with a benção kick. Capoeirista (ii) comes forward with his left leg under her kick.

C Capoeirista (ii) defends himself by attacking Capoeirista (i) with the cabeçada.

D In this example, the cabeçada is performed by placing the top of the head on the mid-part of the opponent's upper body. In this way, the cabeçada is used to knock the opponent off balance.

Rasteira

Rasteira means "to sweep." It is one of the most popular and classic movements in Capoeira. There are many types of Rasteira, but they all have the same purpose—to knock your opponent off balance. It is an important move that can rapidly change the atmosphere of the game. Once a player realizes the danger of a rasteira, he or she needs to be aware that it can happen at any time, and must be prepared to adapt his or her game to prevent it knocking them off balance. It is inevitable, however, that you will take a fall, and fear of the rasteira should not affect the freedom of your game. There is a saying in Capoeira: "Those who have not fallen have never played in the roda."

A   Start in a low position, balancing on your left foot that is slightly raised off the floor. Supporting your body with your right arm, bring your left arm up to the side of your body, and keep your right leg out in front of your body.

B   Transfer your weight by bringing your left leg out to the front, taking your weight on your right arm and right foot. Your left arm should continue to come up to the side.

C   Lower your body down to the floor, without collapsing, and bring your left arm up over your head. Your right arm should be behind your body with a soft elbow and can be lowered down as far as you are able to support your body weight.

D   Place your right arm on the floor, and start to bring your left leg across the floor, creating a sweeping motion. Keep your foot flexed in order to hook your opponent's base leg. Your focus should remain toward your partner.

E   Draw a complete semi-circle with the inside of your foot on the floor. Your foot should be flexed, and your body off the floor the whole time. You are supporting yourself, and controlling the movement with your arms, your right foot, and the momentum of the rasteira.

F   As your left leg completes the semi-circle, use your arms to push yourself up. Come up off the right leg until you are in a small lunge position with your hands on the floor in front of you. Look through your legs and arms at your partner.

G   Swivel the position of your feet around to the front, back to a low position with your weight centered on your back left heel. Your right leg should be relaxed in front. Finally, release the right hand off the floor, and fold it in to protect your face. You are now back to your starting position after completing the rasteira.

H   This is a close-up showing how the foot is used to hook the opponent's base leg with the rasteira. The flexed foot of the rasteira sweeps around to hook the foot of the base leg to sweep the opponent off balance.

I   Rasteira in action: Capoeirista (i) has attacked her opponent with a kick. Capoeirista (ii) has seen the opportunity to use a rasteira with the intention of knocking Capoeirista (i) off her balance.

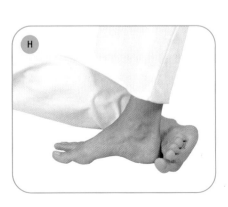

Tesoura

The tesoura ("scissors") is a traditional movement. When performed in a Regional game, it can be quite an aggressive movement that can knock an opponent over by trapping both the legs, leaving no option other than to fall safely. The following tesoura can be found most typically in a game of Capoeira Angola where it can also be used as a trap, but allows the opponent more freedom of movement, adding fluidity and interaction to the game.

A   Start in a low position, balancing on your left foot that is slightly raised off the floor. Support your balance with the right arm on the floor, keep the right leg out to the front with a relaxed knee, and fold your left arm in to protect your face.

B   Bring your left arm up and over your body, and place it on the floor above your head. At the same time pivot around to the right, using your right foot, and start to bring your left leg up and forward.

C   Supporting your body weight with your arms, bring both knees in toward your chest, keeping a forward focus.

D   Bring both your knees together into your chest until you reach a queda de rins position.

E   Extend both your legs out to the floor. Using the support of your arms and feet, keep your hips slightly twisted to the right. Your left heel should be off the floor, and your right foot beginning to plant itself fully on the floor.

F   Push your body up with your arms and slide your feet along the floor, maintaining the direction of your hips, and keeping your legs open. Look over your left shoulder to enable you to maintain eye contact in the tesoura position.

Golpes de Capoeira — Capoeira kicks

Golpes ("kicks") play a huge part in Capoeira. Your training for most of your attacks within the game will come in the form of kicks. There are many varieties of kick within Capoeira, with everything from frontal kicks, side kicks, diagonal kicks, and spinning kicks, to over-head kicks, and low-moving kicks. There is a kick for every direction, and they can come from many starting positions. Some of the kicks in Capoeira Regional were introduced by Mestre Bimba, inspired by other martial arts such as Savate. Many of the kicks, however, can only be found within the Capoeira game.

Kicks can also be incorporated into acrobatic moves. These may include kicking somebody from a bananeira (hand stand), lowering the leg as the opponent approaches to attack with a cabeçada (head butt), or even a flying kick such as the parafuso (screw), which is a jumping combination of the armarda and martelo kicks.

There are kicks in Capoeira that are designed to attack your opponent from every angle. There are kicks to force your opponent backward, sideways, in the air, and to the floor. The delivery of kicks is very important, and the control of speed, height, and distance will be gained through training regularly. A good Capoeirista can perform a kick without his opponent being able to anticipate where the kick is coming from; this type of deceit is common within the Capoeira game. It is important to take care that you have good control over your kicks when playing at this level, as many of these kicks can lead to serious injury. You need to be aware of where your leg is going and its intentions, so it is best to concentrate on and train in the more traditional ways of applying a kick before adding trickery. While training in these kicks, try to start off with a slow speed to achieve the correct technique; it is very important that you concentrate on the balance, control, and base leg of the kick.

Benção

Benção ("to bless") is a frontal kick that is popular in both Capoeira Angola and Capoeira Regional. It can be used to push your opponent away from you, and is usually aimed at the chest of your opponent.

A Start from the ginga position. Your left foot should be forward and your right foot back, with the right arm up protecting your face, and your left arm down at your left side.

B Bring your right leg up from the back to the front by lifting your knee toward your chest. As you bring the knee up, switch over your arm position so that your left arm is in opposition to your knee, thus protecting your upper body. Keep your base leg knee bent to give yourself a good firm base with the supporting leg.

C Keeping your foot flexed, push your foot through the air until your kicking leg is fully extended. As you do this, tilt your pelvis forward, and allow your upper body to counter-balance by tilting slightly backward. Don't forget to maintain a forward focus throughout.

D The benção can be used to push your partner away from you in the roda. The Capoeirista in this example is placing her foot on her partner's chest.

E The Capoeirista shown here is receiving the benção and is escaping using the resistência (see pages 40–41).

F Here is the result of a strong, well-used benção. Notice how the pelvis is tilted forward and the supporting leg has a strong base.

Martelo

The martelo ("hammer") is a lateral kick that is quite similar to kicks used in other martial arts. It is a powerful kick that can be applied to the side of your opponent's upper body and head.

A   Start from the ginga position. The left foot should be forward and the right foot back, with your right arm up protecting your face, and the left arm by your left side.

B   Swivel your left foot to the right, bringing your right knee up. Twist your pelvis around, and switch the position of your arms with your left arm in opposition to the knee that is protecting the body.

C   Extend your leg out with speed from the knee without allowing your knee to drop. Keep your left foot turned out, and your supporting leg slightly bent for a strong base. Your upper body should tilt back slightly to counter-balance, but your shoulders should not fall back. Remember to maintain eye contact.

Chapa

The direct translation of the word chapa means "flat surface;" if you look at the kicking foot, it is angled flat toward the opponent's body. A chapa kick is a front kick that is also lateral to the floor. This kick can be applied to areas at the front of the upper body, from the stomach to the head.

A   Start from the ginga position, with your left foot forward and your right foot back. Your right arm should be protecting your face, and your left arm should be down by your left side.

B   Swivel your left foot to the left, and bring your body around until your pelvis is facing the left side. As you do this, bring your right knee up and switch over the position of the arms so that the left arm is in opposition with the hand protecting your face.

C   Extend your leg fully to the front, keeping it parallel to the floor. Your body should be tilted back slightly to counter-balance the height of your kick, and your supporting left leg should remain turned out. The leg in the chapa does not unfold from the knee, but unlike the martelo, the flexed foot pushes through the air.

Meia lua de frente

Meia lua de frente ("half-moon to the front") is another classic kick of Capoeira, and earns its name because it resembles the shape of a half-moon. It is not only used to hit your opponent, but to also force him or her to go sideways, and play lower to the floor. This kick adds fluidity to the game.

A   Start from the ginga position with your right foot forward and your left foot back. Your left arm should be up protecting your face, and your right arm down your right side.

B   From the ginga position bring your left leg up and across the front of your body around hip-height, with the foot flexed. While your leg comes up and across, the arms switch position with the right arm in opposition to the leg, protecting your body. The knee of your supporting leg remains soft for a strong base.

C   Bring your kicking leg all the way across the front of your body to complete the shape of a half-moon. Notice how the foot of the supporting leg is turned out; this should happen from the start of the kick.

D   Once your half-moon shape is completed, bring your kicking leg down from the end of the half-moon shape to the right side of the body.

E   To finish the kick and return to the ginga, start to fold your left leg back in from your knee.

F   Start to place your left leg back into the ginga position by swivelling your body and supporting foot back to the front. Continue to fold your left leg down and back to the ginga position.

A   Place your left foot, which has completed the meia lua de frente, back into the ginga position. You should now be ready to continue to play.

A   B   C

Quexada

The quexada kick is a powerful and attractive move. It prepares you for other spinning kicks and, when practiced continuously, can be used to improve the speed and control of your leg.

A   Start from the ginga position. Your left foot should be forward, your right foot back, with your right arm up protecting your face, and your left arm down by your left side.

B   Swivel your feet to the right and switch your arm position, with the left arm now protecting your face. Your legs should be in a wide squat position in preparation to kick.

C   Shift your right leg forward to replace your left leg, which in turn lifts off the floor. Your arms should start to open out to switch position, and your base foot should be turned out with a soft knee for a strong base.

D   Fan your left leg up and out to the side, keeping the foot flexed and the body weight central so that you have a good balance. Your arms should now have switched, and the right arm is folded in to protect the body.

F

E   Open your leg fully to the side with your arms open, ready to switch to the ginga position. Allow your left leg to fall straight from this position back to the ginga.

F   This is a quexada in action. The Capoeirista who has just received the quexada is about to give her partner a rasteira. The firm base of the Capoeirista in the quexada will prevent him from falling.

Beija flor

The beija flor ("hummingbird") is a beautiful and impressive kick that can be executed with speed for an effective over-head kick. The beija flor kick is more advanced, and requires balance and control to use it efficiently in the roda. The kick is commonly used within Capoeira shows; the name is inspired by the shape of the movement as the leg can be compared with the beak of a hummingbird. Some groups may refer to this kick as aú batido, which means a cartwheel, with the leg beating the air.

A BEIJA FLOR IN ACTION.

Spinning kicks

Spinning kicks can add speed and dynamics to your game, and are exciting for the spectator. Spinning kicks vary in speed according to the rhythm of the game, and a fast kick can also appear in a slow game.

Armada

This is a spinning kick unique to Capoeira. It develops a student's agility, balance, and focus while he or she is turning at high speed. It is a dynamic and visually very impressive move.

A Start from the ginga position. Your right foot should be forward and your left foot back, with your left arm up protecting your face and your right arm down by your right side.

B Bring your left leg from the back of the ginga position to the side, keeping your arms in the same position, and your body facing the front.

C Step on to your left leg and begin to turn yourself around toward the left shoulder. At this point your hips should be facing to the side. Your arms maintain the same position and your focus remains forward.

D Swivel yourself around toward your left shoulder. During the turn your right foot should be behind and your left foot in front. Your arms should have switched over, with your right arm protecting your face and your left arm to the side. Whip your head around to return focus to the front as quickly as possible.

E Bring the right leg forward and transfer the weight on to your right leg by lifting the left leg off the floor. Bring the focus forward as the upper body starts to face the front, with the left arm leading the way.

F Bring your left leg up from the floor with speed. Keep your base leg knee bent, as your left leg comes up. You are still in the middle of the continuous turn.

G Your left leg comes up from the right to the front of your body like an opening fan. Your base leg knee remains bent and your focus is forward.

H Your leg continues to carry to the side, with your base leg firmly planted on the floor. Your foot should be flexed.

I Your kicking leg comes from the side, straight down to the back to complete the kick by finishing in the ginga position.

Meia lua de compasso or rabo de arraia

Meia lua de compasso ("half-moon of the compass") is compared to a compass used in geometry because the base foot is planted on the floor and the other leg draws a circle in the air around you. In Capoeira Angola this kick is called the rabo de arraia ("tail of the stingray"). It is a low, grounded kick that can be quite dangerous when performed at high speed. If you decide to do the meia lua de compasso with velocity, be very careful since the speed of the heel coming around can seriously injure your opponent, especially if the opponent's reflexes are not fast enough to escape the oncoming kick. This kick should only be practiced with any speed when you are aware of your opponent's ability level, and are confident of your own control.

A   Start from the ginga position. Your right foot should be forward and your left foot back, with your left arm up protecting your face and your right arm down by your right side.

B   Swivel your feet around to the left so that your hips are facing to the side. Your shoulders should face forward and your knees should be bent. Your focus should also remain forward.

C   Place your hands on the floor so that your left arm is placed farther back through your legs, and your right arm is out to the front of your legs. Look through the small gap between your right arm and your right leg toward your partner; at this point the left leg should be straight. Keep your right leg bent in a kind of lunge position.

D   Pivot around on your right leg and allow your hands to move around the floor to assist the pivot. Bring your left leg off the floor and begin to make a circle with the kick.

E   Continue to pivot your base right leg and use the arms to bring yourself around with the head relaxed down. Keep the foot of the kicking leg flexed and your base-leg knee bent. Don't forget to maintain eye contact with your opponent.

F   Continue to move your leg around in a circle by pivoting your base-right leg and using your arms on the floor. Notice how the eye contact has been maintained throughout.

G   Bring yourself upright and lower your left leg to the back in the ginga position.

Meia lua de compasso with cocorinha

A   Capoeirista (i) applies the meia lua de compasso. Capoeirista (ii) uses the cocorinha to escape the oncoming kick.

Martelo de chão

Martelo de chão ("hammer kick on the floor") is a low kick that is not only used to kick, but also to force the opponent to escape, bringing color and fluidity to the game. Due to the fact that Capoeira has lower, more grounded games, this kick is used when both of you are in a low game. It is a martelo kick that is adapted for the lower game.

A   Start in a low position sitting over your left foot. The heel should be raised off the floor, and you should be balanced on the ball of your foot. Keep your right leg out to the front with a soft knee. Place your right hand on the floor to support your balance, and bring your left arm into the air with the elbow bent. Keep your focus forward.

B   Lower yourself to the right by bending your right arm in so that the elbow comes in to the right side of your body. Bring your left arm farther up above your head, and start to move your body off your left heel.

C   Lower your body fully to the right, tuck your elbow in above your hip, and place your left arm on the floor in front of your head. Start to bring your back leg off the floor, and don't forget to maintain eye contact.

D   As you bring your left leg up and over to the front, lower your head to the floor, and keep the elbow well into the side of your body. Keep the left hand in a strong position on the floor to support yourself.

E   Keep the same position, and bring your left leg over, aiming toward the floor to the right.

F   Allow your left leg to come down to the floor, and bring yourself up by using your arms and legs. Keep the elbows supple, and maintain eye contact throughout.

G   Transfer your weight over to your left leg and straighten the right. Start to move your focus around to the right, and bring your right arm off the floor to protect your face.

H Come up, and swivel your legs and body to face the front in the ginga position with your arms and legs. Bring your right arm down to your side, and your left arm up to protect your face.

I Martelo de chão ("martelo on the floor") in action.

Training combinations

The following training combinations have been put together to enable you to incorporate some of the moves learned in this chapter. By practicing these sequences you will begin to gain an understanding of how to interact with your partner using attack and defense moves. These sequences are to be practiced with two people and represent Capoeira in action.

Saida do berimbau

Saida do berimbau means "leaving the berimbau." At the start of a Capoeira game, both Capoeiristas crouch down in front of the berimbau. When they have been given permission to commence play, they shake hands as a sign of respect, and usually enter the roda performing the aú (cartwheel) movement.

A   Crouch down in front of the berimbau and shake hands with your partner, making eye contact.
B   Both Capoeiristas prepare to enter the roda with the aú movement, still maintaining eye contact.
C   When performing the aú, the Capoeiristas need to be facing each other. Do not enter the roda with your back to your opponent.
D   Both Capoeiristas descend from the aú movement into the ginga, ready to commence the game. This is not a rule, but a suggestion.

Meia lua de frente with cocorinha

This basic combination will enable you to understand the use of cocorinha in escaping oncoming kicks. Training in the cocorinha with meia lua de frente will also start to prepare you for escaping spinning kicks, such as meia lua de compasso and armada.

A   Starting from the ginga position, one of the Capoeiristas applies a meia lua de frente with the right leg.
B   The meia lua de frente is completed while his opponent escapes it using a cocorinha.

Meia lua de frente with negativa recuada

As previously described, negativa recuada is an escape that enables you to move on the ground. This training exercise will teach you to escape by moving backward while you are low to the ground.

A   Capoeirista (i) and Capoeirista (ii) start mirroring each other from a ginga position.

B   Both Capoeiristas ginga from left to right. During the ginga, Capoeirista (ii) begins to prepare himself to apply a meia lua de frente.

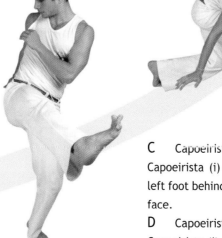

C   Capoeirista (ii) applies a meia lua de frente. Capoeirista (i) goes down towards the floor with the left foot behind, bringing the left arm up to protect the face.

D   Capoeirista (ii) completes the meia lua de frente. Capoeirista (i) escapes with a negativa recuarda.

Meia lua de compasso with cocorinha

In this combination you will gain an understanding of the power of meia lua de compasso. Make sure that you train for this exercise close together and that the kicking leg is not much higher than the head of the person who is defending. The person escaping with the cocorinha needs to come in close and under the kick, with his or her head just below the knee of the oncoming kick. The power of the kick is in the foot, so coming in closer will keep the defending Capoeirista in a safer place.

A   Both Capoeiristas start by facing each other in a ginga position, with the left foot behind and the left arm folded across to protect the face.

B   Both Capoeiristas step out to the side with the back leg.

C   Capoeirista (ii) starts to apply the meia lua de compasso kick, turning counterclockwise, and maintaining eye contact. Capoeirista (i) goes into the cocorinha position, to escape the oncoming kick.

D—E Both Capoeiristas maintain their eye contact while Capoeirista (ii) completes the meia lua de compasso kick.

On completion of the meia lua de compasso kick, both Capoeiristas return to the ginga position.

C   Capoeirista (ii) lifts his left leg off the floor and begins to execute the meia lua de compasso, turning anti-clockwise. Capoeirista (i) lifts his right leg off the floor, turning clockwise. Capoeirista (ii) is slightly farther ahead in the movement than Capoeirista (i). As the leg of Capoeirista (ii) starts to pass over Capoeirista (i), Capoeirista (ii) follows with his meia lua de compasso.

Meia lua de compasso with rasteira

In this combination it is very important to ensure that your rasteira sweep moves in the same direction as the oncoming kick. A common mistake made by beginners is to move against the kick, thus leaving themselves vulnerable to attack.

A   Capoeirista (ii) applies the meia lua de compasso. Capoeirista (i) escapes it and attacks Capoeirista (ii) by using the rasteira.

Meia lua de compasso training

This exercise should be practiced in pairs starting at a moderate pace. It should be performed continuously and speeded up once you are comfortable with the move. It is common to feel dizzy while practicing this move. If you experience dizziness, stop and rest before continuing with the exercise. It is important to warn your partner that you are about to stop since stopping abruptly can cause accidents. You should never underestimate the power of a meia lua de compasso—even when performed at a slow speed this kick can cause serious injuries. Timing and precision are vital in order to master this combination and to ensure your safety.

A   The Capoeiristas start by facing each other in a ginga position, with the left foot behind and the left arm folded across to protect the face.

B   Both Capoeiristas move into the preparation position for the meia lua de compasso, turning toward the back leg. Their hands are placed on the floor and eye contact is maintained.

Chapa with resistência

This exercise will give you a better understanding of how to move backward while escaping. At the end of the resistência make sure that you return to your game swiftly.

A   Both Capoeiristas start by mirroring each other in the ginga position, Capoeirista (i) with the left leg back, and Capoeirista (ii) with the right leg back.

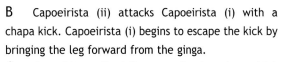

B   Capoeirista (ii) attacks Capoeirista (i) with a chapa kick. Capoeirista (i) begins to escape the kick by bringing the leg forward from the ginga.
C   Capoeirista (ii) fully extends the chapa kick toward her opponent's head. Capoeirsta (i) escapes the kick using the resistência. From this position Capoeirista (i) could quite easily go down to the floor and add a rasteira, or simply connect a ground movement, such as a rolê, in order to continue the game.

Quexada training

This exercise should be practiced in pairs, starting at a moderate pace. It should be performed continuously and only speeded up when you feel comfortable with the move. This exercise is the best way to teach a Capoeirista to escape from fast spinning kicks, as your defense is not on the floor, and you can counter-attack easily. It is also teaches you to move toward your opponent while he is kicking. Ensure that you maintain eye contact, and that your head is slightly backward, which will make your esquiva more efficient.

A   Both Capoeiristas start with their feet parallel with their left foot in front. They maintain eye contact even though they are facing different directions.

B   Capoeirista (i) brings his right leg behind his left leg to prepare to apply the quexada. Capoeirista (ii) anticipates the kick by escaping with a small esquiva, transferring the weight over to his right leg.

C   Capoeirista (i) applies the quexada kick with his left leg. Capoeirista (ii) escapes the kick with an esquiva to the right, leaning slightly backward.

D   Capoeirista (ii) starts his quexada kick by bringing his right leg forward toward the left leg. Capoeirista (i) begins to escape the kick, transferring the weight over to his left into a small esquiva.

F   Capoeirista (ii) brings the leg higher into the quexada kick, maintaining eye contact. Capoeirista (i) lowers down into the esquiva. This low position also allows him to prepare to apply a quexada with his other leg. These quexadas can be practiced continuously, and are a good way of building up velocity and improving your stamina.

Aú with cabeçada

This exercise should be practiced in pairs, with each Capoeirista taking turns in each position. It is a great way to improve your ability to defend, since you are being attacked while you are upside down. You are not simply focusing on your balance, but also on your opponent who is moving in to head butt you. Make sure that you keep close to your opponent and, once mastered, you will be able to add fluidity and interaction. Don't forget that when applied in a game, the cabeçada may be applied with some force, resulting in a fall. You must learn to recover from such a fall by using a queda de quatro or queda de três (pages 54–55).

A   Start by facing your partner in a low, crouched-down position.

B   Capoeirista (ii) places his left hand on the floor and begins to transfer his weight over to the left side, bringing the right arm up.

C   Capoeirista (ii) begins to move into the aú (cartwheel). Meanwhile, Capoeirista (i) places both hands on the floor and prepares himself to give a cabeçada (head butt).

D   Capoeirista (ii) performs the aú movement, keeping his focus forward toward his partner. Capoeirista (i) moves in to give his partner a cabeçada in the stomach.

Benção, resistência with tesoura and aú

This is a more complex exercise involving the skills of both attack and defense. As you move into this combination, make sure you maintain eye contact. It is common for a beginner to focus on attack and defense, but to lose concentration and eye contact during the more fluid movements of the sequence, such as the tesoura and the aú. This is also a combination that starts high and finishes on the ground. Once complete don't forget to come up again into the ginga.

A   Capoeirista (i) starts the benção kick by bringing his left leg up. Capoeirista (ii) begins to lean back in the resistência.

B   Capoeirista (i) applies a full benção kick toward his opponent. Capoeirista (ii) goes back into a resistência to avoid the oncoming kick.

C   Capoeirista (ii) lowers himself down to the floor to the queda de rins on his left elbow, with the right hand on the floor for support.

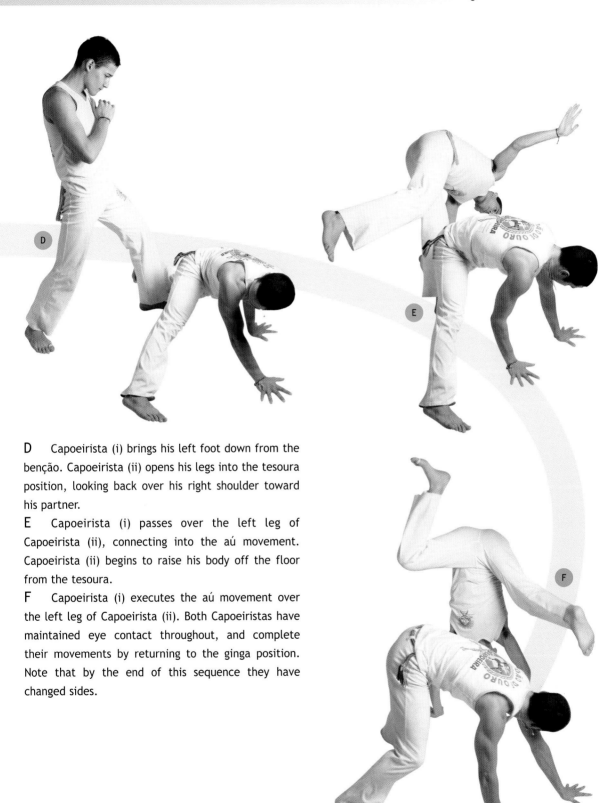

D   Capoeirista (i) brings his left foot down from the benção. Capoeirista (ii) opens his legs into the tesoura position, looking back over his right shoulder toward his partner.

E   Capoeirista (i) passes over the left leg of Capoeirista (ii), connecting into the aú movement. Capoeirista (ii) begins to raise his body off the floor from the tesoura.

F   Capoeirista (i) executes the aú movement over the left leg of Capoeirista (ii). Both Capoeiristas have maintained eye contact throughout, and complete their movements by returning to the ginga position. Note that by the end of this sequence they have changed sides.

Martelo with rasteira em pé

This exercise trains you for the rasteira from a standing position. The rasteira em pé ("sweep from standing") simply means that the rasteira does not go all the way to the floor. This move should be practiced in the same direction as the oncoming kick. Both Capoeiristas should take turns to practice both of the movements on each side.

A   Both Capoeiristas start in the ginga position. Capoeirista (i) has his left leg back, and Capoeirista (ii) is mirroring his partner with his right leg back.

B   Capoeirista (ii) brings his back leg from the ginga position, and begins to apply the martelo kick with his right leg. Capoeirista (i) brings his back leg from the ginga position, and begins to apply a rasteira to the base leg of Capoeirista (ii).

C   Capoeirista (ii) completes the martelo kick while Capoeirista (i) knocks the base leg of Capoeirista (ii) with the rasteira, with the intention of taking him off balance.

Both Capoeiristas return to the ginga position. From here the Capoeiristas ginga to change legs and repeat the exercise with the other leg.

Final notes on training combinations

As mentioned in the previous pages, maintaining eye contact is an important part of your training. I normally tell my students that if you are not focusing on each other and interacting, there is no point in practicing combinations. Before beginning the sequences, ensure that both you and your partner are ready by doing some of the exercises shown in the warm-up section (pages 26—33). This can be followed by a five-minute ginga. Once you have learned the combinations, you should start to train in a more playful way by mixing, creating, and improvising. These combinations provide a bridge from exercises to the actual game. Use the steps that come naturally to you, and do not simply use the moves as though they are dance steps. You are not engaging in a solo performance—the most important part of the game is the interaction.

Strength, balance, and flexibility

The training exercises in this book will improve your strength, balance, and flexibility. In the art of Capoeira, these three components put together will increase your range of movement, and allow you to move more freely within your game, while also improving your stamina. Stamina is an important asset within the roda, enabling you to play to the best of your ability for longer periods. Flexibility, meanwhile, will improve the efficiency of attacks, escapes, and the execution of advanced moves. Balance will add control and beauty to the execution of your moves, and minimize the possibility of falling. Strength will decrease the possibility of injury and is the basis of flexibility, precision, and balance. A well-rounded Capoeirista will strive to attain a good level of balance, strength, and flexibility, and will not neglect any of these three aspects of training.

B

A

Exercises to strengthen the upper body

Mergulho

You will find mergulho ("to dive") used in most Capoeira classes. It may seem impossible at first, but with time you will see an improvement in your upper-body strength and flexibility.

A Start on all fours with your legs open wide and your knees straight.

B Lower yourself down to the floor, keeping your elbows in and your upper body slightly off the ground. Do not rest your body on the floor.

C   Straighten your elbows, and push your upper back up.

D   Lower your upper body back down to the floor, and then push yourself back up with your arms.

Return to the starting position, stretching out your lower back. Repeat this movement several times.

Exercise for queda de rins

Many movements within Capoeira involve leaning and balancing with your elbow in the side of your body. This can feel uncomfortable at first, but once you gain sufficient upper-body strength to support yourself with the elbow in the correct position, you will find it beneficial to assist you in perfecting the moves. Queda de rins ("fall onto the kidneys") is demanding, but with dedication and daily practice you will soon feel the benefits. It will help to increase your movement facility and bring an increased fluidity to your game.

A　Start with your legs apart and your hands on the floor in front of your body, keeping your back straight.

B　Move your weight over to your arms as you start to bend in the right knee.

C　As you continue to bend your right knee in, keep the leg straight. Lower your upper-body weight to the floor by bending your elbows, bringing your right elbow into your right side just above your right hip. As you lower yourself down, turn your head to the left. Do not allow any part of your body to touch the floor. Hold this position for a couple of seconds.

D　Return to the starting position by using your arms to push your body away from the floor, and straighten your right knee. Once returned to the starting position, repeat the exercise on the other side.

Ponte training

Ponte ("bridge") is a basic movement that can be performed on its own. Practicing ponte will improve a whole range of movements, and helps to add fluidity to your game. There are many moves within Capoeira that will benefit from training in the ponte.

A   Lie flat on the floor with your knees bent, and your feet shoulder-width apart. Place your hands up above your head with your palms flat on the floor, and your fingers pointing toward your shoulders.

B   Push your hands into the floor, and raise your pelvis to the ceiling. Start to bring your head and body off the floor.

C   Achieve the full ponte by using your arms to push your pelvis up as far as you can, allow your head to relax back, and your legs to straighten. Don't forget to keep the knees soft.

Backbend training

This movement must be practiced with two people and will help you to gain confidence in moving while you are upside down. It will also improve your judgment as to when your hands should reach the floor in backward movements, and will increase your control, balance, and flexibility.

A   Capoeirista (i) secures his partner by the wrists with a wide stance and relaxed knees. Capoeirista (ii) stands straight, lifting her arms above her head.

B   Capoeirista (i) brings his upper body forward, keeping his knees bent and securing his partner firmly by her wrists. Capoeirista (ii) allows her partner to lift her body back as he bends forward. At this point her feet are coming off the floor.

C   Capoeirista (i) keeps hold of the wrists and, bending the knees, brings the upper body down to the floor, and places his partner's hands on the floor.

D   Capoeirista (ii) allows Capoeirista (i) to place her hands on the floor and start to lift her left leg up.

E   Capoeirista (i) straightens his legs and allows his partner to complete her movement. Capoeirista (ii) now has her focus forward and is allowing her left leg to go toward the floor, with her lower back still resting on her partner for support. Capoeirista (i), although supporting his partner less, must be aware of his partner's balance before letting go. Capoeirista (ii) allows her left foot to find the floor, and brings the rest of her body over. At this point her fellow Capoeirista has let go, but is still close by.

F   Capoeirista (ii) brings both her feet to the floor, bringing her legs over, and finishes with the feet parallel.

G   Both Capoeiristas finish by rolling through the spine to a standing position.

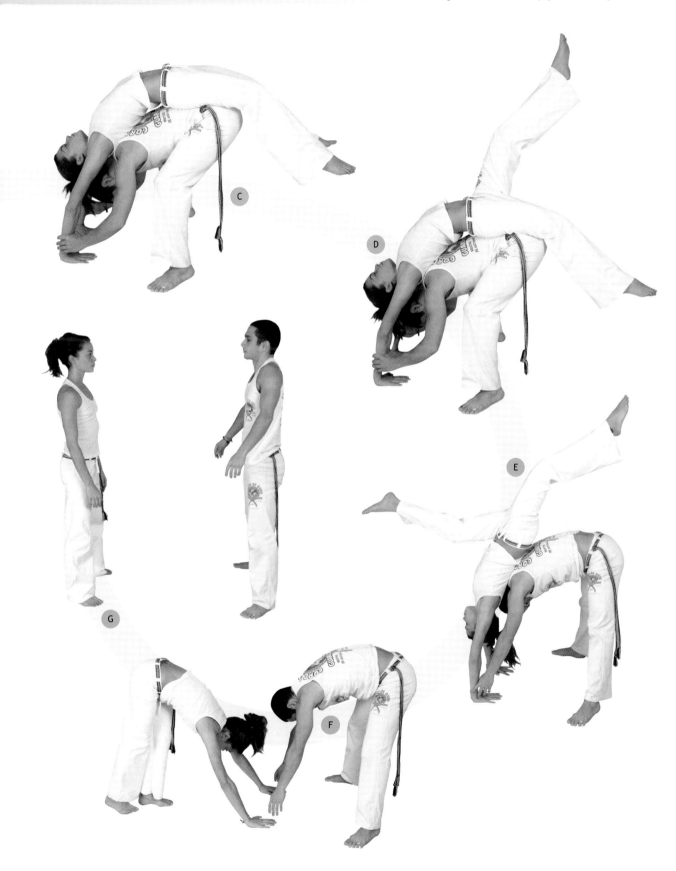

Practicing the bananeira

There are many forms of the bananeira ("hand stand"). Once you have mastered the simple bananeira, you can be creative and play around with your balance. Capoeiristas who are comfortable with their balance can perform the bananeira with one hand. This, in turn can evolve, with the Capoeirista jumping and turning on one hand. This turn is referred to as pião de mão ("turn on one hand"). It is also quite common for Capoeiristas to walk around the roda on their hands. There are also bananeiras that involve leaning the body over in different directions, such as performing a back bend in the bananeira. These are impressive balances, and a great demonstration of strength and flexibility.

Always keep the focus forward, as more often than not, there will be a cabeçada (head butt) coming your way to test your balance. Cabeçada is the chosen mode of attack when performing a bananeira as it is bad etiquette to kick your opponent's arms, body, or head while he or she is balancing in this move.

For a simple bananeira, you can start by practicing with a partner holding your legs for support and balance, or against a wall. Once you start to practice the bananeira alone, take care that there is nobody behind you, and that you have plenty of space.

Bananeira training exercise

A Capoeirista (ii) starts in a standing position holding his partner by the right ankle. Capoeirista (i) keeps both hands on the floor, looking toward his partner, with the right leg lifted off the floor.

B Capoeirista (ii) comes in toward his partner and secures his partner's ankle with both hands.

C Capoeirista (i) lifts his left leg off the floor while his partner is securing his right leg, taking the weight in both hands on the floor.

D Capoeirista (i) brings his left leg toward the ceiling, while keeping his focus toward his partner.

E Capoeirista (i) straightens his left leg toward the ceiling and concentrates on his balance in this position, while his partner keeps him in balance by securing his right leg. When the balance is found, his partner can remove his grip to test the balance, but be ready to catch his partner if he starts to fall. To release, Capoeirista (i) returns his left leg to the floor.

F   An important factor of the bananeira is to focus forward toward your partner. Many people start to practice it looking at the floor, but it is vital that you start to train for the bananeira with your head relaxed and the top of your head pointing toward the floor. This way you will still be able to see what is happening within the game.

More creative examples of the bananeira

It is likely that you will see many different varieties of bananeiras being performed by the more advanced students within the roda. Here are a few examples of bananeiras taking different forms within the balance.

A This bananeira involves excellent balance and shoulder strength.

B The lower part of the body has been lowered down from the lower back and the left leg kept bent in while the right leg is stretched out toward the floor.

Ponte de bananeira
(a bridge from a handstand)

A   Capoeirista (i) goes up into a hand stand, keeping her focus forward. Capoeirista (ii) secures his partner by holding both ankles.

B   Capoeirista (ii) then turns around until he is back-to-back with his partner, continuing to secure his partner's ankles firmly.

C   Capoeirista (ii) begins to squat in a wide stance. As he is squatting he takes the weight of his partner's body over his back with a firm grip, being sure to keep his partner in balance. It is very important that he keeps a straight back as he goes down, and is in a deep squat to avoid back injury. You should never arch your lower back in this position.

D   As Capoeirista (ii) bends forward, he brings his partner over his back. The hands of Capoeirista (i) leave the floor and she allows her partner to place her feet on the floor.

E   Capoeirista (i) gains her balance with the help of her partner, and then brings her upper body up to a standing position to complete the movement.

Aú de cabeça

Aú de cabeça ("cartwheel on the head") is a type of cartwheel, but because you have your head on the floor, it is classed as a ground movement rather than an acrobatic movement. Aú de cabeça is a common movement within a game of Capoeira Angola and the Muidinho game of Cordão de Ouro. It is a beautiful movement that an advanced student can perform by removing their hands from the floor, and balancing on the top of his or her head. It is also a stylish movement, which, when added to your game, will allow you to move around the roda.

A Start in a low position with your weight resting on your back left foot and your right leg out to the front. Supporting your balance with your right hand on the floor, bring your left arm up to the side, keeping your focus forward.

B On your right foot, pivot around to the right, bringing your back foot off the floor, and allowing the left arm to come over and join your right hand on the floor. Don't forget to keep your focus toward your partner.

C Place the top of your head on the floor and bend your elbows so that your arms are in a good position to support your body. Continue to lift your left leg off the floor.

D Balancing on your head, bring your left leg up, and at the same time, start to bring your right leg off the floor.

(Continued)

E

F

(Continued)

E   Bring your right foot off the floor, using your arms and your head to maintain a steady balance.

F—G Bring your left foot down to the floor first, and then allow the right foot to follow to finish the movement.

H   As your right foot comes down to the floor, swivel your feet and body to face the front by bringing your right foot to the back. Pivot on your back foot to return to the starting position, with your right foot behind you and your left foot in front. It is important that you maintain eye contact with your partner throughout the movement.

G

H

THE MUSIC

Music is a central and essential part of Capoeira, setting it apart from other martial arts. This traditional element of Capoeira is one that most groups strive to uphold. It is perhaps the use of music within Capoeira that leads to the common confusion about whether it is a fight or a dance. The music sets the tempo and style of the roda, whether it's an Angola game or a fast and dynamic Regional-style fight. Music within Capoeira encourages the fluid movements of the Capoeiristas, and enables them to keep time. The use of music also encourages a sense of belonging, where students sing together as they watch others play. Within the roda, work and commitments can be left outside; the powerful music of Capoeira helps students to do this. Without the music of the bateria (orchestra) one cannot experience true Capoeira.

The bateria is at the heart of every roda. It is usually made up of three main instruments: the berimbau (a monochordal musical bow), the pandeiro (tambourine), and the atabaque (drum).

The berimbau

The berimbau is sometimes referred to as the soul of Capoeira, and is often used as the symbol of the art. Mestres have been known to say that the berimbau is the real mestre of the roda, and its importance cannot be underestimated within Capoeira. Learning to play the berimbau is an important part of a Capoeirista's training, especially for those aiming to progress in the art.

The emergence of the berimbau within Capoeira is in dispute, but what is certain is that it originated from Africa. This musical bow was originally used to accompany storytelling, poetry, and chants. The berimbau is one of the oldest known instruments. Modern versions are made up of a single string from the wire of a used car tire which is attached to a wooden bow. The bow is made from biriba, a strong yet flexible wood that provides a good shape and powerful sound. A cabaça (a hollowed gourd) is attached to the bottom of the bow and serves to amplify the sound.

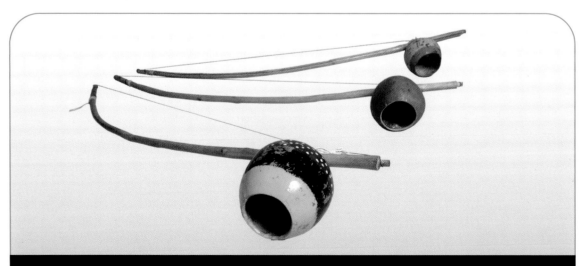

THE THREE BERIMBAUS: VIOLA (TOP), MEDIO (MIDDLE), AND GUNGA OR BERRA BOI (BOTTOM), WITH CABAÇAS THAT INCREASE IN SIZE.

opposite MESTRE PONCIANINHO PLAYS THE ATABAQUE, A TALL DRUM MADE FROM COWHIDE.

There are three main types of berimbau within the bateria: the gunga, the medio, and the viola. The gunga, or the berra-boi, performs the role of the bass, and is the most dominant sound in the bateria. Its function is to keep time and constant rhythm. The medio follows the basic beat, but can also produce variations on the theme. The viola provides a variation on the beat, but adds a wilder element to the music.

The role of the berimbau is extremely important in the roda, musically and ritualistically. Before a game commences it is traditional for Capoeiristas to crouch at the foot of the berimbau, as it is this instrument that sets the rhythm and tone of the game. The game can be playful, aggressive, fast, or slow, its tempo and mood are dictated by the particular "toques" (rhythms) being played. Different toques are used for different styles of Capoeira. There are different toques for different regions and are created by particular mestres, reflecting their own style and personalities. Capoeira Regional, for example, has seven main rhythms: São Bento Grande, Cavalaria, Luna, Banguela, Santa Maria, Idalina, and Amazonas.

The berimbau is usually played by an experienced Capoeirista who holds an important position within the roda. Some claim that it is impossible to learn the art of Capoeira without the berimbau, as it encourages a keen sense of timing. It also signifies the beginning and end of a game, and warns Capoeiristas when a game is becoming too heated. The rhythm acts as a language and form of instruction. Historically, particular rhythms were also used to warn Capoeiristas that the cavalaria (police) were approaching. Although beautifully painted berimbaus can be found in many tourist locations in Brazil, it is important for a Capoeirista to find an instrument that has been made with love or make one for themselves.

Percussion instruments

Percussion instruments are also used within the bateria. With the exception of the pandeiro (tambourine) most of the percussion instruments used within Capoeira derive from central and western Africa.

A CABAÇA (TOP) AND A CAXIXI (BELOW), BOTH PART OF THE BERIMBAU.

The instrument is played by holding the bow in the left hand alongside a pebble or a coin. The pressure of the pebble on the wire produces varying notes. The berimbau is not plucked with the hand, but is played with a stick known as the baqueta. The baqueta is held in the right hand along with a small woven rattle called a caxixi, which is filled with dried beans or, more traditionally, with rosary beads. When shaken, the caxixi of wicker and beans or beads produces a soft sound, and adds another dimension to the soulful string of the berimbau.

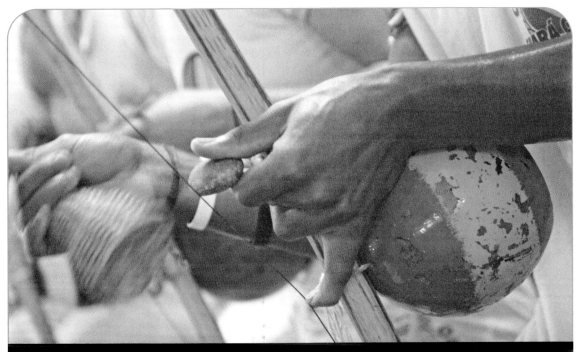

A PEBBLE OR COIN IS HELD AGAINST THE STRING OF A BERIMBAU TO CREATE DIFFERENT NOTES.

THE BATERIA IS AN INTEGRAL PART OF THE CAPOEIRA EXPERIENCE AND IS AT THE HEART OF EVERY RODA.

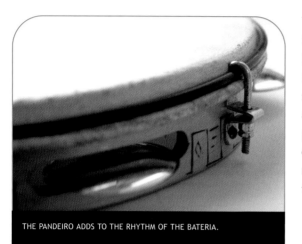

THE PANDEIRO ADDS TO THE RHYTHM OF THE BATERIA.

The pandeiro (tambourine) was introduced to Brazil by the Portuguese settlers. It is often played with four beats and a shake. Other instruments include a reco reco (a gourd carved with notches and played with a slim stick); an agôgô (a double-gonged bell); and an atabaque (tall drums made from cowhide that are played with the hands like bongos). Each Capoeirista contributes to the music of the roda; if he or she does not play an instrument they can simply use their hands to clap the rhythms.

THE AGÔGÔ, A DOUBLE-GONGED BELL, AND AN ATABAQUE, A TALL DRUM PLAYED WITH THE HANDS.

The songs of Capoeira

Songs and chants are extremely important in Capoeira. They add to the atmosphere of the roda and encourage a sense of community within the group. They reflect the culture of Brazil in general, and the history of Capoeira in particular. The themes of the songs range from history to religion, and can serve to deliver teachings and philosophies. They can be used to comment on the game in hand, or to relate tales of famous teachers from the past.

There are several different types of song used in Capoeira. The "ladainha" (litany) is sung at the beginning of the roda. Traditionally sung by a soloist, the lyrics demand a response that is sung by the rest of the group who make up the chorus. The mestre will sing of his experiences, or use the ladainha to challenge another player with a provocative song.

Ladainhas derive from Capoeira Angola. This example was written by Mestre Pastinha.

Iê maior é Deus

(God is greater)

Pequeno sou eu

(I am small)

O que eu tenho foi Deus que me deu

(Everything I have, God gave to me)

O que eu tenho foi Deus que me deu

(Everything I have, God gave to me)

Na roda de Capoeira grande pequeno sou eu

(In the roda of Capoeira I am both great and small)

The ladainha is usually followed by the chula, or louvação. This is a call-and-response song where Capoeiristas repeat the words of their mestre word-for-word. The third type of song is the corrido. These songs can be sung during the game. The chorus remains constant and is repeated several times, but the soloist can be spontaneous and it can be used to provide a running commentary of the game, or to tell a story.

Oi, Sim, Sim, Sim

(Yes, yes, yes)

Oi, Nao, Nao, Nao

(No, no, no)

Oi Sim, Sim, Sim

(Yes, yes, yes)

Oi, Nao, Nao, Nao

(No, no, no)

Mas hoje tem, amanha no

(Today there is)

Mas hoje tem, amanha no

(But tomorrow there is not)

Oi, Sim, Sim, Sim

(Yes, yes, yes)

Oi, Nao, Nao, Nao

(No, no, no)

Olha a pisada de Lampião*

(The steps of Lampião)

Oi, Sim, Sim, Sim

(Yes, yes, yes)

Oi, Nao, Nao, Nao

(No, no, no)

* Lampião was a famous outlaw from the northeast of Brazil in the 1900s.

AN AGÔGÔ BEING PLAYED IN THE RODA.

Eu não sou daqui

(I am not from here)

Marinheiro só [chorus]

(Only a sailor)

Eu não tenho amor

(I don't have love) [Repeat chorus]

De São Salvador

(I am from St. Salvador) [Repeat chorus]

O marinheiro, marinheiro

(O sailor, sailor) [Repeat chorus]

Quem te ensino a nada?

(Who taught you how to swim?) [Repeat chorus]

Ou foi o tombo do navio

(Or was it the rocking of the ship) [Repeat chorus]

Ou foi o balanço do mar

(Or was it the sway of the ocean) [Repeat chorus]

Lá vem lá vem

(Here he comes) [Repeat chorus]

Lá vem ele vindo

(There he is coming) [Repeat chorus]

Todo de branco

(All in white) [Repeat chorus]

Com seu bonézinho

(With his little hat) [Repeat chorus]

Vou dizer minha, mulher, Paraná*

(I will tell my woman, Paraná)

Capoeira me venceu, Paraná

(That Capoeira conquered me, Paraná)

Paranáe, paranáe, Paraná

(Paranáe, paranáe, Paraná)

Ela que bateu o pe firme, Paraná

(She wanted to kick hard, Paraná)

Isso nao aconteceu, Paraná

(This did not happen, Paraná)

Paranáe, paranáe, Paraná

(Paranáe, paranáe, Paraná)

O Paranáe, paranáe, Paraná

(O Paranáe, paranáe, Paraná)

Paranáe, Paraná

(Paranáe, Paraná)

Paranáe, paranáe, Paraná

(Paranáe, paranáe, Paraná)

Assim dera que o morro, Paraná

(This way the mountain, Paraná)

Se mudou para a cidade, Paraná

(Moved to the city, Paraná)

Paranáe, paranáe, Paraná

(Paranáe, paranáe, Paraná)

Tem batuque todo dia, Paraná

(There is drumming every day, Paraná)

Mulata de qualidade, Paraná

(And fine women, Paraná)

Paranáe, paranáe, Paraná

(Paranáe, paranáe, Paraná)

One of the most famous songs in Capoeira is a corridos that celebrates the place Paraná. The chorus remains constant, but the words in between can be improvised, reflecting the spontaneous nature of a Capoeira game.

* Paraná is a famous Brazilian river and state where the war of the Triple Alliance took place. Many Capoeiristas were said to have fought and died in this war.

Capoeira as performance

One of the unique qualities of Capoeira as a martial art is that it is entertaining to watch. Not only do the high kicks and back flips leave spectators dumbfounded, the dynamic interaction between the Capoeiristas can also leave watchers on the edge of their seats. Will they collide or knock each other out of the roda? Are they simply playing, or will things get nasty? A good Capoeira show will provide excitement, tension, and above all demonstrate the humor common to all good Capoeiristas. The expressive nature of the art draws out the personality of the Capoeiristas, and audiences appreciate that they are not simply watching a series of exercises. The element of music and song, and the fluid and beautiful movements that this inspires, also enable it to be used in a performance context.

The performance of Capoeira is not a recent development; Capoeiristas of the nineteenth century would also perform tricks for enthusiastic onlookers. During the 1930s and 1940s, demonstrations of Capoeira in Brazil were performed for visiting foreign dignitaries, and it has often been used in folkloric shows to promote Afro-Brazilian culture.

The performance element of Capoeira has often been criticized for its reliance on flashy acrobatic moves and its crowd-pleasing tendencies. It is argued that this emphasis on acrobatics detracts from the spontaneous nature of the game, especially when the shows are choreographed for extra effect. Although a Capoeirista cannot learn the true art simply by performing, it may be that many a serious Capoeirista first came into contact with Capoeira in a performance context. If Capoeira was not performed in such a way, the beauty of its moves would not be shared with such a wide public. Through performance, the beauty of the art has touched and inspired many.

CAPOEIRA IS ONE OF THE GREAT PERFORMANCE ARTS AND CAN BE MESMERIZING TO WATCH.

THE GAME

The roda and the jogo

Although moves and theories can be taught by a Capoeira mestre, real Capoeira cannot be learned until these movements are experienced within the roda. Before Capoeira was taught within academies, the roda was the place a student learned Capoeira. Through interaction with their opponent in the frenzy of a game, a student of Capoeira would learn the hard way through trial and error. Observation was also a large part of Capoeira, as students would spend many weeks watching the moves of other Capoeiristas in the roda. It is also a place where a mestre can learn about his students, as the way a student reacts within a roda reflects his or her personality and progress.

The roda takes place within a circle made up of Capoeiristas and the bateria, and Capoeiristas take turns to enter the middle of the circle. The roda will traditionally begin with slow Angola rhythms and will continue to pick up speed as the game progresses. Capoeiristas will clap and sing as those in the middle play, building the energy until it reaches an almost electric pitch. A true Capoeirista does not enter the roda to win a game, but to enjoy being part of the game. It is for this reason that the roda can accommodate both a gentle game between father and son, or a fiery game between two experienced Capoeiristas.

The roda is a place of fair play; a place to learn as well as to fight. A Capoeirista will be unable to use a pre-prepared sequence of moves and must practice what he has learned by means of trial and error. The game of Capoeira (jogo) is seen by many Capoeiristas to reflect life. Capoeira is not simply a physical sport, but also places much emphasis on the spiritual and psychological side of the game, often referred to as "malandragem," or "malicia." Malandragem is used to describe the knowledge of human nature, which can be put into practice in the roda in the form of shrewdness, cunning, and wariness. A Capoeirista can use malandragem to pre-empt another's moves, or to trick an opponent into believing he will attack in a certain way. At the last minute, he may change direction and surprise both his opponent and the rest of the roda. A Capoeirista can use these skills to outwit his or her opponent, and it enables older mestres to surprise younger students as it does not rely on physical strength, but guile. Experience within Capoeira often wins out against the speed and flexibility of youth.

The roda teaches you to live a better life, and the challenges you face within the roda will teach you to be a wiser person in everyday life. As Mestre Bimba would say, "You are better off being beaten within the roda than in the streets." In other words, the roda is a safer place to make mistakes, both on physical and psychological levels. The roda teaches you to keep a level head and to control your ego. Mestre Pastinha would say that the best Capoeiristas are the calm and more centered students. It is in the roda that your strengths and weaknesses are highlighted. The roda is a place to express yourself, and you can tell a lot about a Capoeirista by how he or she plays in the roda; all training in Capoeira leads to the roda.

Hierarchy

Although all students of Capoeira play within the roda, there are varying levels. The first level is the beginner. At this level, Capoeira is a hobby, and although the student may work hard in training, they tend to focus mainly on the physical aspects of the game. If a student persists with the training to the second level, they will hopefully begin to see that there is more to Capoeira than the moves, and start to gain an understanding of malicia, the music, and the history of the art. The

opposite CONTRA-MESTRE CASQUINHA (LEFT) EVADES MESTRE PONCIANO'S ARMADA WITH A PERFECTLY TIMED "RAIZ" CARTWHEEL.

BARIS YAZAR PERFORMS A "PARAFUSO" FLYING KICK. PARAFUSO MEANS "TWIST" OR "SCREW."

Capoeirista should become more shrewd and expressive in their play, and understand that the interaction and the game are more important than simply winning or losing. The third level is that of the mestre. Capoeira is not simply a leisure activity at this stage, but a way of life. The mestre still plays Capoeira, but has a greater understanding of the game, and a responsibility for others within the roda.

The mestre

As in many martial arts, the mestre in Capoeira is a position that commands respect; the mestre has an understanding of all aspects of Capoeira and a commitment to share his knowledge with others. The title of mestre should be passed on from another mestre, to ensure that the standard of Capoeira is upheld, and that its traditions are carried forward. Even when awarded this title, mestres should continue to be supervised by their own mestre, ensuring that standards are maintained. The knowledge of the mestres is well respected within Capoeira and they often travel around the world, sharing their experience and styles with other groups. Even for the mestre, however, the knowledge of Capoeira is never-ending. The more they learn, the more they discover what they do not know.

The mestre is in control of the roda, directing the speed of play with the berimbau. He is also responsible for calming a game if it becomes too heated. The mestre has the responsibility for ensuring the physical well-being of his players. A rough game is only acceptable between equals. Any visiting Capoeiristas must respect the rules laid down by the mestre of the group.

Different mestres practice different forms of etiquette within the roda. A saying often used in Capoeira is "Know where you step." In other words, you should learn and respect the customs of the group you are playing with. For example, there are different ways of entering the roda, different songs, and various styles of uniform. Angoleiros often wear shoes, and in my group, for example, bare chests are not permitted. A Capoeirista must also observe the style of the group, and be mindful of whether they practice a tough or

MESTRE JOSE ANTONIO KNEELS AT THE "PÉ DE BERIMBAU" (THE FOOT OF THE BERIMBAU) TO SING A LADAINHA.

STUDENTS TRAIN EN MASSE AT A CAPOEIRA EVENT.

delicate game. It is also important to note that a level of discipline exists within a roda that distinguishes it from a dance class. It is a martial art, and players cannot simply move in and out of the roda to have a sip of water or to talk.

Respect for the mestre also extends to a respect for the differing styles and methods within Capoeira. This respect enables all styles to flourish, thus preserving individuality and beliefs. Capoeira has the room and flexibility for varying styles and growth, and I believe this makes the art unique.

The grading system

Although Capoeira is steeped in tradition, you will never attend two classes that are exactly the same. Different schools vary how they grade their students, and the belts they award to their students. The system you will find outlined here is the one I follow in Cordão de Ouro in London.

Batizado

The first step that one of my Capoeiristas will take towards achieving their first belt is attending a batizado (baptism). The batizado was created last century by Mestre Bimba to grade students. It is a grading ceremony, and symbolizes your true start as a Capoeirista. As the mestre, I will award someone's grade according to their level of discipline, skill, knowledge, and musicality shown in class. The batizado is a happy occasion, and resembles a celebration where a belt may be awarded. Because Capoeira is not simply a physical game, the mestre may withhold a belt if the student does not have the right mental attitude. A teaching grade, for example, cannot be awarded to someone who is too aggressive or egotistical, as this may be dangerous for those he goes on to teach. The belts awarded within Cordão de Ouro are as follows:

Belt one: green

It is at this grade that the Capoeirista attends his first batizado, which is, in effect, his initiation into the art. It is also during a Capoeirista's first batizado that he or she can choose a godfather. This can be a friend or special person in the world of Capoeira. The godfather is often the one who presents the belt. To achieve this belt, the student must have knowledge of the basic moves, kicks, and escapes from kicks. He or she must have a basic understanding of the game, the etiquette of the roda, and learned how to fall correctly.

Belt two: green and yellow

At the second level, a student must have a greater understanding of the different styles of Capoeira: Angola, Regional, and Miudinho. He or she must also have a basic knowledge of the instruments played within the roda.

Belt three: yellow

By the third belt, the student must have learned the eight sequences of Mestre Bimba. They should also be able to play the instruments competently, and be able to sing within the roda, not simply as part of the chorus, but at solo level.

THE MESTRE LEADS A CHILDREN'S CLASS IN SONG. HE IS HOLDING A "PANDEIRO" (TAMBOURINE) WHICH HE USES TO SET THE RHYTHM.

Belt four: yellow and blue

By this stage, the Capoeirista must have a deeper understanding of the styles within Capoeira. He or she must display more expression within the game and show an understanding of Miudinho. A student will also be expected to visit Brazil at least once to gain an understanding of the cultural roots of Capoeira. They will be expected to sing while playing the instruments, demonstrating a higher level of co-ordination. It is at this stage that the Capoeirista will sing the ladainha.

Belt five: blue

At this grade, the student is approaching the instructor grade. He or she will be assessed on general knowledge and whether or not they will pursue Capoeira as a career. They will also be expected to begin to teach within the group to gain experience.

Belt six: green, yellow, and blue

This grade is the "formado" (teacher). In order to gain this belt, the student must present a sequence of advanced movements. He or she will be asked to play a typical Angola, Regional, and Miudinho game, and be able to demonstrate a "cintura desprezada" (a sequence devised by Mestre Bimba involving acrobatic throws), that demonstrates falling and landing skills.

A VOLTÃO MUNDO (SIMILAR TO A FORWARD WALKOVER).

AN IMPROBABLE ACROBATIC CONTORTION IS USED TO EVADE A CHARGE.

Belt seven: green, yellow, blue, and white

This belt is the contra mestre belt (one level below mestre). A student must have experience of teaching. At this grade the Capoeirista will be judged not only on his or her own skill and ability, but by the work they do with their students.

Belt eight: green and white

The mestre belt.

Belt nine: yellow and white

Mestre belt, second degree.

Belt ten: blue and white

Mestre belt, third degree.

Belt eleven: white

The Grand Mestre belt. This is the highest grade in Capoeira. The Grand Mestre will supervise other mestres.

Final words to the beginner

Although I have been practicing Capoeira for 22 years, there are times when I still feel like a beginner. For me, Capoeira is still a constant challenge. It is an amazing art, helping individual to develop into stronger, healthier, and more focused people. In this art you have to fight your insecurities, your fears, your anger, and much more besides. These qualities are what have kept me going.

I was quite young when I started training in Capoeira, but it didn't take me long to know that I had something in my life that would be there forever. Capoeira becomes like your skin and not some fashion accessory that you can change. Personally, it brings me closer to my ancestors and keeps me in contact with my roots. The music of Capoeira can take you to a spiritual level, and there is nothing quite like being in a Capoeira roda with your friends and surrounded by the bateria. The music excites you, and as you start to interact, the game can take many forms, shapes, moods, and levels of danger. For me, Capoeira has all the elements one needs: our job as Capoeiristas is to mix them correctly.

As my life challenges change, my Capoeira challenges may also change. I have been teaching Capoeira in the UK for the past six years, and this experience has shown me how my belief in the art can change other people's lives. Teaching Capoeira is a real challenge because it has such a rich culture, and so many aspects that are not easy to demonstrate, or to put into words.

The physical aspects may be a real challenge for many, but the hardest skill to perfect in Capoeira is to develop the feeling and expression within your game. For my students it is no different. This challenge is probably one of the things that keeps most people coming back, and the journey can be as enjoyable and rewarding as the destination. In the process of becoming a better Capoeirista, you can learn so much about yourself. You will learn about your weaknesses and your strengths, and that is a great discovery to make about oneself. I hope this book has the power to inspire you in this new path, and helps you to achieve your own goals.

MESTRE PONCIANO AND MESTRE JOGO DE DENTRO PLAY A BEAUTIFUL GAME OF CAPOEIRA ANGOLA.

GLOSSARY

AGÔGÔ	Double-gonged cow-bell	CHAPA	Thrusting side kick
AMAZONAS	Berimbau toque within Capoeira	CHULA	Song
ANGOLEIRO	Practitioner of Capoeira Angola	CINTURA DESPREZADA	Series of acrobatic movements
APELIDO	Nickname		involving two Capoeiristas;
ARMADA	Spinning kick		designed by Mestre Bimba to
ATABAQUE	Drum		help students lose their fear of
AÚ	Cartwheel		flipping in the air
AÚ BATIDO	Type of kicking cartwheel	COCORINHA	Small, squatting, defensive
AÚ DE CABEÇA	Grounded cartwheel on		movement
	the head	CONTRA-MESTRE	One level before master
		CORDÃO DE OURO	Belt of gold
BAHIA	State in Brazil	CORRIDOS	Song
BANANEIRA	Hand stand		
BANGUELA	Toque within Capoeira	DESEQUILIBRANTES	Unbalancing techniques
BAQUETA	Stick to play berimbau	DICIPULO	Capoeira student/disciple
BATERIA	Orchestra		
BATIZADO	Grading ceremony	ESQUIVA	Escape movement
BEIJA FLOR	Type of upside-down kick, liter-	ESQUIVA BAIXA	Low escape movement
	ally meaning "hummingbird"	ESQUIVA LATERAL	Sideways escape movement
BENÇÃO	Type of kick		
BERIMBAU	Monochordal musical bow	FAVELA	Shanty town
BERRA-BOI	Large, low-pitched berimbau;	FORMADO	"Formed" or graduated student
	also known as gunga		
BIRIBA	Wood used to make berimbau	GINGA	Basic sway-like movement; the
			foundation step in Capoeira
CABAÇA	Hollowed gourd found	GOLPES	Kicks
	on berimbau	GRAND MESTRE SUASSUNA	Grand master and founder
CABEÇADA	Head butt		of Cordão de Ouro
CABEÇEIROS	Practitioner of the head butt	GUNGA	Type of berimbau; another
CAPA	Basket worn on head to carry		name for berra-boi
	birds to the market		
CAPOAEROBICS	Aerobic workout	IDALINA	Berimbau toque within Capoeira
	using Capoeira moves	IUNA	Berimbau toque within Capoeira
CAPOEIRA ANGOLA	Style of Capoeira denoted by		to which only formados and
	Mestre Pastinha		above may play
CAPOEIRA REGIONAL	Style of Capoeira created by		
	Mestre Bimba	JOAO GRANDE	Famous master of Capoeira
CAPOEIRISTA	Person who plays Capoeira		Angola
CAVALARIA	Berimbau toque used as warning	JOAO PEQUENO	Famous master of Capoeira
	that police were nearby		Angola
CAXIXI	Wooden rattle	JOGO	The game

GLOSSARY

JOGO DE DENTRO	The inner game	PONTE	Bridge
KIPURA	To flutter	QUEDA DE QUATRO	Fall on to all fours
		QUEDA DE RINS	Fall on to the kidneys
LADAINHAS	Songs sung at the beginning of the roda	QUEDA DE TRÊS	Fall on to three limbs
		QUEXADA	Type of front kick aimed at the chin
LOUVAÇÃO	Song	QUILOMBOS	Fugitive slave villages
MALANDRAGEM	Cunning behavior		
MALICIA	Guile	RABO DE ARRARIA	"Stingray's tail;" a low, grounded kick
MARTELO	Type of kick		
MARTELO DE CHÃO	Spinning kick from the ground	RASTEIRA	Sweeping movement
MEDIO	Medium-sized type of berimbau	RECO RECO	Percussion instrument
MEIA LUA DE COMPASSO	"Half-moon in a compass;" 360° spinning kick with hands placed on floor	RESISTÊNCIA	Backwars-bending escape movement
		RODA	Circle in which Capoeira is played
MEIA LUA DE FRENTE	"Half-moon in front;" classic circular front kick	ROLÊ	Rolling escape movement
MERGULHO	Strengthening exercise		
MESTRE	Master grade in Capoeira	SAIDA	Exit or escape
MESTRE BIMBA	Founder of Capoeira Regional	SANTA MARIA	Toque within Capoeira
MESTRE PASTINHA	Master of Capoeira Angola	SENZALAS	Slaves' quarters
MIUDINHO	Style of Capoeira developed by Mestre Suassuna	SÃO BENTO GRANDE	Toque within Capoeira
		TESOURA	Scissors take-down
NEGATIVA	Low escape movement	TOQUE	Rhythm played on berimbau
		TUPI	Native Brazilian people
PANDEIRO	Tambourine		
PARAFUSO	Spinning, jumping kick	VIOLA	Small, high-pitched type of berimbau
PASSA PESCOÇO	Variation of queda de rins		
PIÃO DE MÃO	Handspin		

PHOTOGRAPHIC CREDITS

All photography by Mike Holdsworth, with the exception of those supplied by the following photographers and/or agencies (copyright rests with these individuals and/or their agencies):
Ponciano and Louise Almeida: front cover, 2, 8, 11, 14, 16, 20, 115, 119-21, 122, 123
Shanta Bhavnani: 5
Isabelle Schoenholzer: 9, 13, 15, 117
Paul West: 6, 22-23, 34-35, 43

MAKING CONTACT

INTERNATIONAL CAPOEIRA ORGANIZATIONS

AUSTRIA

- TRIMM-FIT
Gesundheit & Spass durch
Bewegung, Hessenplatz 12,
4020 Linz, Austria
- E-mail: xuxocdo@hotmail.com
- Website: www.xuxocdo.com

BRAZIL

- CORDÃO DE OURO
Mestre Suassuna
Rua Jesuino Pascoal, n.44
Santa Cicilia, CEP 01224-050
São Paulo, Brazil
- E-mail: bocarica@terra.com.br
- Website: www.grupo
cordaodeouro.com.br

- CORDÃO DE OURO
Contra-Mestre Boca-Rica
Av. Diógenes Ribeiro de Lima,
n.2000 Alto de Pinheiros, Brazil
- E-mail: bocarica@terra.com.br
- Website: www.bocarica
capoeira.com.br

- CORDÃO DE OURO
Mestre Espirro Mirim
Rua Manaus, 878-Henrique jorge,
CEP 6052-200, Fortaleza-Ceara,
Brazil
- E-mail: espirromirim@
hotmail.com
- Website: www.geocities.com/
colosseum/park/4170

FRANCE

- ASSOCIATION CORDÃO DE
OURO CDO
Contra-Mestre Chicote
79, rue des Entrepreneurs,
75015 Paris, France
- E-mail: cdo.paris@yahoo.fr
- Website: www.cdoparis.com

- CAPOEIRA MALICIA
Contra-Mestre Zangado
Marseille, France
- E-mail: capoeirazangado@
bol.com

- GROUP SENZALA CAPOEIRA
Mestre Sorriso
3 rue Lakanal, 34090
Montpellier, France
- E-mail: capoeira@association
senzala.com
- Website: www.association
senzala.com

NETHERLANDS

- CORDÃO DE OURO
Mestre Espirro Mirim
Enschede, Netherlands
- E-mail: info@capoeira-cdo.nl
- Website: www.capoeira-cdo.nl

UK

- CORDÃO DE OURO
Mestre Poncianinho & Contra-
Mestre Casquinha
57 Bembridge House, Iron Mill
Road, London, SW18 2AQ, UK
- Email: info@cdol.co.uk
- Website: www.cdol.co.uk
- CORDÃO DE OURO
Contra-Mestre Parente
Central Youth Centre, Walker
Street, Kensington, Liverpool, UK
- Email: parentecapu@
hotmail.com
- Website: www.cordao-de-
ouro.org

- CORDÃO DE OURO
Contra-Mestre Parente
St John's Church Hall, St John's
Road, Old Trafford, Manchester,
M16 7QX, UK
- Email: parentecapu@
hotmail.com
- Website: www.cordao-de-
ouro.org

- GROUP SENZALA CAPOEIRA
Professor Tasmania
Dance City, Temple Street,
Newcastle Upon Tyne,
NE1 4BR, UK
- Email: jimi@groupsenzala.
co.uk
- Website: www.groupsenzala.
co.uk

INTERNATIONAL CAPOEIRA ORGANIZATIONS

- GROUP SENZALA CAPOEIRA
Contra-Mestre Pedro
CityLife House, Sturton Street,
Cambridge, CB1 2QF, UK
  - Email: info@cambridge-capoeira.co.uk
  - Website: www.cambridge-capoeira.co.uk

USA
- INTERNATIONAL CAPOEIRA
ANGOLA FOUNDATION
Mestre Cobra Mansa
733 Euclid Street NW,
Washington, D.C. 20001, USA
  - Tel: 001-202-332-0828
  - Website: www.capoeira-angola.org

- CAPOEIRA ANGOLA CENTER OF
MESTRE JOÃO GRANDE
104 West 14th Street,
New York, NY 10011, USA
  - Tel: 001-212 989 6975
  - Website: www.joaogrande.org

- CORDÃO DE OURO
Contra-Mestre Denis
Illinois Disciples Foundation, 610
E Springfield Avenue, Champaign,
IL 61820, USA
  - Email: cordaodeouro@gmail.com
  - Website: www.cdoillinois.com

- UNITED CAPOEIRA
ASSOCIATION
Mestre Acordeon
CapoeiraArts, 2026 Addison
Street, Berkeley, CA 94704, USA
  - Tel: 001-510-666-1255
  - Website:
www.capoeiraarts.com

- CORDÃO DE OURO
Contra-Mestre Marisa
2909 N Milwaukee Avenue,
Chicago, IL 60618, USA
  - Email: gingarte_capoeira@yahoo.com
  - Website: www.capoeira.uchicago.edu

- CORDÃO DE OURO
Mestre Virgulino
1423 Central NE, Albuquerque, NM
87106, USA
  - Email: seriacdo@hotmail.com
  - Website: http://166.70.211.128/info/schools/pg_view/id_10393524/

USEFUL WEBSITES

An extensive site featuring a list of all mestres, song lyrics, videos, and a large knowledge base.
- wwwcapoeira4all.com

The science of the art of Capoeira.
- www.capoeirascience.com

Historical documents relating to Capoeira.
- www.capoeira-palmares.fr/histor/index_en.htm

Capoeira videos, music, and downloads.
- www.capuraginga.com

The largest Capoeira community on the internet.
- www.capoeira.com

Links to the United Capoeira Association Schools.
- www.capoeira.bz

Capoeira clothing, music, videos, instruments, and books.
- www.capoeiraarts.com

accidents 22
aerobic exercises 56
agôgô 112
Antonio, Mestre 20
armada 76-7
atabaque 17, 109, 112
aú de cabeça 104-7
aú with cabeçada 89

back stretch 57
backbend training 97-8
balance 93-107
bananeira 97-103
bateria 17, 108
batizado 120
Batuque 17
beija flor 75
belt grades 120
belts, how to tie 24-5
benção 69
benção, resistência with tesoura
    and aú 90-1
berimbau 108-10
Bimba, Mestre 12, 14-17
bless 69
Brasilia, Mestre 19
Brazil 10-13
breathing 56-7

cabaça 108
cabeçada 62-3
calf stretch 57
"Capoeira" 12
Capoeira Angola 11, 13, 14,
    17-19
Capoeira Regional 12, 14-17, 18
chapa 71
chula 113
cocorinha 36
commandments 14
Cordão de Ouro 19-20

dance 10
defense moves 40-51
development 12-21
drums 17
dynamic stretches 56

entertainment 115
escape moves 40-51
esquiva 40-3

falling 53-5
flexibility 56-61, 93-107

game, the 116-23
ginga 14, 17, 34-5
golpes 68-81
grading system 120
grappling techniques 17, 18

green and yellow belt 120
green belt 120
Grupo de Capoeira Angola
    Pelourinho 18-19
gunga 110

hammer 70
hamstring stretch 59
head butt 62-3
hierarchy 116-20
high kicks 18
hips, warming up 30
history 11-13

inner game 18, 19
inner-thigh stretches 32, 57-8

jogo 116
jogo de dentro 18
joint rotations 56

kicks 68-81
knees, warming up 30

ladainha 113
leg stretch 60
levels 116-20
louvacao 113
lunges 32

malandragem 14, 116
malicia 116
martelo de chão 80-1
martelo kick 70
martelo position 60
martelo with rasteira em pé 92
martial art 10
medio 110
meia lua de compasso 78
meia lua de compasso training
    86-7
meia lua de compasso with
    cocorinha 79, 85
meia lua de compasso with
    rasteira 86
meia lua de frente 72-3
meia lua de frente with
    cocorinha 82-3
meia lua de frente with
    negativa recuada 84
mergulho 94-5
mestre, the 119-20
Miudhino 19-20
music 8, 17, 18, 108-14

neck, warming up 26-8
negativa 44-51
negativa 2 47-9
negativa recuada 50-1

observation 116

pandeiro 112
Paraná 114
passa pescoço 39
Pasthina, Mestre 12-13, 17-19,
    20, 113, 116
percussion instruments 110-12
performance element 115
Ponciannho, Mestre 8, 13, 20,
    108
ponte training 97

quadriceps stretch 60-1
queda de quatro 54
queda de rins 37-8, 96
queda de três 54-5
quexada 74-5, 88

rabo de arraia 78
rasteira 64-5
resistência 40-1
respect 120
rises 31
roda 116
rolê 52-3
rules of conduct 17

saida do berimbau 82
self-defense 10, 12
sequências 17
shoulder stretch 61
shoulders, warming up 26-8
side stretches 33, 57-8
slavery 11-12
songs 113-14
spinning kicks 76-81
static stretches 56
strength 93-107
stretches
    flexibility 56-61
    warming up 32-3
Suassuna, Grande Mestre 19-20

tesoura 66-7
tocques 20
training 17, 22
combinations 82-92
    warming up 26-33
Tucano, Mestre 13

uniforms 17, 18
upper-body strength 94-5

viola 110

warming up 26-33
women 20
wrists, warming up 29

yellow belt 120